THE TWEEN GIRLS PUBERTY HANDBOOK

Understand Your Bodily Changes, Emotions, Menstruation, Nutritional Needs and Don't Let Social Media Ruin Your Body Image

KIM CRANSTON

© **Copyright 2024 - All rights reserved.**

The content within this book may not be reproduced, duplicated or transmitted without direct written permission from the author or the publisher

Under no circumstances will any blame or legal responsibility be held against the publisher, or author, for any damages, reparation, or monetary loss due to the information contained within this book. Either directly or indirectly. You are responsible for your own choices, actions, and results.

Legal Notice:

This book is copyright protected. This book is only for personal use. You cannot amend, distribute, sell, use, quote or paraphrase any part, of the content within this book, without the consent of the author or publisher.

Disclaimer Notice:

Please note the information contained within this document is for educational and entertainment purposes only. All effort has been expended to present accurate, up-to-date, and reliable, complete information. No warranties of any kind are declared or implied. Readers acknowledge that the author is not engaging in the rendering of legal, financial, medical or professional advice. The content within this book has been derived from various sources. Please consult a licensed professional before attempting any techniques outlined in this book.

By reading this document, the reader agrees that under no circumstances is the author responsible for any losses, direct or indirect, which are incurred as a result of the use of the information contained within this document, including, but not limited to, — errors, omissions, or inaccuracies.

Table of Contents

Introduction	7
1. INTRODUCTION TO PUBERTY	13
What Is Puberty? An Overview	14
The Science of Growing Up: Hormones and How They Work	15
Early Birds and Late Bloomers: Why Timing Varies	17
Your Body's Timetable: Understanding Your Unique Puberty Schedule	20
Pop Quiz	22
2. PHYSICAL CHANGES	25
Breast Development: What to Expect and When	26
The Lowdown on Body Hair: Managing New Growth	29
Navigating Growth Spurts: Tips and Tales	30
Pop Quiz	33
3. MENSTRUATION 101	37
Your First Period: What It Is and How to Prepare	37
Understanding Your Body's New Rhythms: Basic Anatomy and Menstruation	37
Preparing for Your First Period	38
Managing Expectations: Flow, Duration, and Symptoms	39
Emotional Readiness: Embracing the Change with Confidence	39
Respecting Privacy and Boundaries	40
Choosing Period Products: A Guide to What's What	40
Period Kits for School: What to Include	44
Tracking Your Cycle: Why and How	45
Busting Period Myths	48
Pop Quiz	50
4. PERSONAL CARE AND HYGIENE	53
Puberty and Hygiene: Keeping Clean and Confident	53
Dealing with Acne: Skincare during Puberty	56

Hair Care: Managing Changes in Hair Texture and Volume	58
Hygiene for Private Areas: Caring for Your Changing Body	60
Pop Quiz	62

5. HEALTHY LIFESTYLE CHOICES — 67
Mindful Eating: Nutrition and Puberty	67
The Power of Exercise: Finding Fun in Activities You Love	71
Stress Reduction Techniques for Tweens	74
Getting Enough Sleep: Tips for Restful Nights	77
Pop Quiz	80

6. EMOTIONAL ROLLERCOASTER — 85
Feeling All the Feels: Navigating Emotions during Puberty	85
Anger and Frustration: Healthy Ways to Cope	88
Fill up Your Victory Jar	91
Body Image: Loving Yourself through Changes	93
Pop Quiz	95

7. FRIENDSHIPS AND RELATIONSHIPS — 99
Changing Friendships: Growing Apart and Together	99
Finding Your Support Circle: Peers, Family, and Beyond	102
The Role of Siblings during Puberty: Allies or Annoyances?	103
Communicating with Parents and Adults: Tips for Open Conversations	105
Pop Quiz	107

8. CREATING YOUR PERSONAL PUBERTY DIARY—A SPACE FOR THOUGHTS AND QUESTIONS — 109
Benefits of Journaling	109
What to Include	110
Reflecting on Growth	111
Homework	111

9. NAVIGATING SOCIAL MEDIA AND DIGITAL COMMUNICATION — 113
Social Media: Understanding Its Impact on Self-Image	115
Critical Media Literacy	116

Deep Dive: Social Media and Body Image	118
Impact of Text Messaging and Emails	119
Setting Boundaries: Healthy Habits for Social Media Use	121
Pop Quiz	123
10. BULLYING AND PEER PRESSURE	**127**
Recognizing Bullying and Peer Pressure	127
Strategies for Responding	129
Building Resilience	130
Supporting Others	131
11. BUILDING CONFIDENCE AND SELF-ESTEEM	**133**
Self-Talk for Self-Esteem: How to Be Your Own Cheerleader	133
Celebrating Uniqueness: Embracing Individuality	135
Role Models: Finding Your Inspiration	137
Conclusion	139
References	143

Introduction

Have you ever wondered why your body is changing? What's going to change next? Why are your friends around you changing? Why does it seem like all your friends' faces are suddenly looking down at their phones? Should your face be in a phone? What are you missing? Why do your emotions seem like a rollercoaster? Or how do you tackle the flood of information on social media about growing up (if you are on social media)? You're definitely not alone! Many girls your age are asking the same questions and looking for trustworthy answers. That's exactly why this book exists—to help you navigate all the twists and turns of puberty with confidence and clarity.

Hello! I'm thrilled to walk this journey with you. As someone deeply passionate about supporting girls like you, I wanted to gather accurate, understandable, and relatable information to help you through this significant phase of your life. Remember, there's no right or wrong way to experience puberty, and there are no bad questions. This book is a safe space for all your thoughts and queries.

This handbook is designed just for you—to answer your questions, ease your concerns, and celebrate your growth. We'll explore everything from the physical changes in your body to the emotional ups and downs that might catch you by surprise, along with how nutrition and exercise can impact you at this time in your life. We'll also dive into how to handle the digital world, including texts, emails, and the influence of social media, which can be pretty overwhelming. We'll talk about periods, from what exactly is happening inside your body to how to use period products, and yes, you absolutely can go swimming during your period (we'll talk about this more later in the book)!

I promise to keep our conversation open and inclusive. Whether you're just starting to notice changes in yourself or your friends or you're right in the middle of puberty, this book is for you. You'll find easy-to-understand explanations and practical and actionable advice. Plus, there are fun quizzes, and I encourage you to jot down notes, questions, or anything you're feeling in the margins—think of this book as your personal journal and guide.

As we turn each page together, I encourage you to keep an open mind and actively participate. Think about your own experiences, jot down your thoughts or questions, and don't hesitate to revisit any topic as many times as you need. You will see me use the term "completely normal" a lot in this book. I do this because I had no idea what normal was when I was growing up and going through my puberty journey. What I now know is that there is no normal! Puberty is not a race; it's a personal journey unique to every girl.

As we embark on this adventure together, remember that every question you ask, every feeling you explore, and every piece of knowledge you gain is a step toward becoming the confident and informed young person you are meant to be. Let's embrace this exciting time of discovery and growth together, with lots of learning, laughter, and support along the way.

Ready to start this amazing journey? Let's go!

Welcome

ONE

Introduction to Puberty

Do you remember the first time you rode a bike? At first, it might have seemed a little scary and unpredictable, but with time, practice, and maybe a few falls, you got the hang of it. Even if you don't remember, you probably ride a bike with complete confidence now, right? Puberty can feel like learning to ride a bike—new, challenging, but also a major step toward growing up. Just like you didn't learn to ride a bike overnight, your body doesn't change all at once. It's a series of changes, each important and unique to you.

In this chapter, we're going to explore what happens during puberty. You'll learn about the physical and emotional changes that are part of growing up. Think of this chapter as your guide to understanding these changes and knowing what to expect. It's perfectly normal to have lots of questions and even some worries about all the new things you're experiencing, and that's exactly what we're here to talk about.

What Is Puberty? An Overview

Defining Puberty

Puberty is a major phase in your life when your body starts to develop from a child's into an adult's. This isn't just about getting taller or needing a new bra; it's your body's way of preparing for adulthood, including the ability to reproduce. But it's not just physical—puberty affects your emotions and thoughts, too.

Signs and Symptoms

You might already know some signs of puberty, like getting your period or suddenly finding that your clothes are too small. But there are other signs too, such as growing hair in new places (like under your arms and around your private parts), your breasts developing, and changes in the shape of your body, like wider hips. Boys will have changes, too, like a deeper voice and facial hair. These changes happen over time, not all at once, and everyone has their own pace.

The Universal and Unique

It's important to remember that while everyone goes through puberty, it doesn't look or feel the same for everyone. Some girls start developing breasts as early as eight years old, while others might not start until they're 13 or older (I was 16!). And both are completely normal. The timing and order of these changes are different for everyone, and your genetics influences them. So, if you're curious about when things might start happening for you, it might help to ask your family members when they noticed these changes in themselves.

Psychological Aspects

As your body begins to change, so will your emotions. You might feel super happy one minute and then suddenly feel sad, shy, sulky, or angry the next. These mood swings are a completely normal part of puberty, thanks to the new hormones kicking in. It's really important during this time to notice your moods, show yourself some grace, continue to be kind to others, and don't bottle up anything inside. Talking about your feelings with friends, family, or even a counselor can be really helpful. Keeping a journal can also be a great way to deal with these new emotions, giving you a private space to express yourself and make sense of your feelings.

Reflect and Record

To help you track and understand your feelings during puberty, why not start a personal journal? Use it to write down any changes you notice, how you feel from day to day, and any questions you might have. This can be your private space, just for your thoughts and feelings, and you might find it useful to look back on as you grow. We will talk more about this later in the book.

The Science of Growing Up: Hormones and How They Work

This is a technical section about hormones, the endocrine system, and the brain, but stick with me here. Imagine your body is a high-tech company with a communication network that sends messages to keep everything running smoothly. This network uses special messengers called hormones, which travel through your body to tell different parts what to do and when to do it. During puberty, these hormones are like the managers in the company, making sure that all the big changes you're going through happen just right.

Hormones, like estrogen and testosterone, play leading roles in this process. You've probably heard of these hormones before but might not know exactly what they do. Estrogen is often called the "female hormone" because it's crucial for developing female physical features like breasts and for regulating the menstrual cycle. Testosterone, often known as the "male hormone," is linked to male physical features like facial hair and a deeper voice, but guess what? Both hormones are found in everyone, just in different amounts. During puberty, your body starts producing more of these hormones, which signals your body to start changing into its adult form.

The changes these hormones trigger are pretty impressive. For instance, estrogen helps hips widen and breasts develop, while testosterone can cause the voice to deepen and muscles to grow more pronounced. But their job isn't just about physical changes. These hormones also have a big say in how you feel from day to day. Have you ever felt a sudden mood swing or felt unusually emotional without knowing why? Well, you can often thank these hormonal changes for these new, sometimes confusing feelings.

Now, let's talk about the endocrine system, which is like the headquarters of hormone production. This system includes glands like the pituitary gland, which is often called the "master gland" because it sends out signals to other glands to produce hormones. When the pituitary gland releases its hormones, it tells other parts of your body to make hormones like estrogen and testosterone. It's all interconnected and controlled by this system, ensuring that the right amount of each hormone is released at the right time.

Besides the physical changes and the mood swings, hormones can affect other behaviors. For instance, you might find yourself wanting more independence yet also craving those little things your parents might have done when you were little. Or, maybe you're starting to think differently about friendships and relationships. This can feel a bit overwhelming and confusing, but it's all part of growing up and finding out who you are. Hormones are powerful, and they can influence how you think and feel in many ways. As you navigate through these changes, it's important to remember that feeling a range of emotions during puberty is completely normal, and everyone goes through it, even if it feels like you're on a wild roller coaster at times. The important thing is to talk to a trusted adult to help you get through these constant highs and lows.

As you learn more about how your body works, you might start to notice patterns in your mood or behavior and understand that these are just part of the changes your body is going through. This knowledge can make the whole experience a little less confusing. And remember, if you ever feel overwhelmed by these changes, it's okay to talk about it with someone you trust, like a family member, a teacher, or a counselor. They can help you understand what's happening and why, giving you more confidence as you grow.

Early Birds and Late Bloomers: Why Timing Varies

Isn't it interesting how some of us start to see changes in our bodies at different times? Some girls might start to develop breasts or get their first period earlier than most of their friends, while others might feel like they're waiting forever to catch up (did I mention I was 16?). This variation is perfectly normal, and there are several reasons why puberty might kick in earlier for some and later for others. Truthfully, I struggle even with the terminology of "early bird" and "late bloomer" because it puts a label on something that no one can control. Therefore, there is no "early" or "late" time period. It arrives precisely when it means to, so it's all right on time.

First, let's talk about genetics, which play a huge role in determining when you'll start puberty. Just like you might inherit your mom's curly hair or your dad's freckles, the timing of your puberty can also be inherited. If your mom or your aunts started their periods early, there's a good chance you might, too. On the other hand, if they told you stories about how they were always the last among their friends to go through changes, you might experience something similar. Genetics are like a behind-the-scenes director, guiding the timeline of your body's development. This information is really powerful in helping guide you through your timeline.

But it's not just about genetics—your physical health also influences when puberty begins. Nutritional intake is a major player here. Your body needs a variety of nutrients to kick-start puberty, and lacking essential vitamins and minerals can delay its onset. For instance, girls who are heavily involved in sports might experience a later onset of puberty if their intense physical activity levels lead to lower body fat, which is closely linked to when puberty starts. It's like your body saying, "Hey, let's make sure we have enough resources before we start this major project of growing up."

Speaking of resources, the environment you grow up in also has its part to play. Factors like your overall lifestyle, the level of stress you experience, and even how much you exercise can influence when puberty hits. It's a complex interplay of elements, with your body carefully listening to both internal and external signals to decide the perfect time to start these changes.

Now, let's address the emotional rollercoaster that can accompany being an early bird or a late bloomer. It can feel quite isolating if you're the first one in your class to need a bra or, conversely, if you're the last one still waiting for your growth spurt. You might feel exposed or even different, but remember, puberty is neither a race nor a competition. Everyone's body has its own schedule, which doesn't make anyone better or worse. My younger sister, who got her period when she was 14, told her friends for over a year that she had her period so she wouldn't have to talk about being behind everyone else. This happens a lot.

Teasing or feeling left out can be hurtful, so having a good support system is crucial. First, teasing someone for something over which they have no control doesn't make any sense anyway (as your grandma always said, "If you have nothing nice to say, then don't say anything at all"), but having friends and family who understand what you're going through can make all the difference. If you find yourself being teased, try to express how it makes you feel to someone you trust (fact: being teased hurts). Sometimes, people don't realize the impact of their words until it's clearly communicated. Surround yourself with friends who support you, uplift you, and make you feel good about yourself, no matter what stage of development you're in.

And remember, if you ever feel overwhelmed by these feelings, talking to a trusted adult can provide comfort and perspective. They've been through it, too, and can often reassure you that what you're experiencing is completely normal and temporary. They might share their own stories of dealing with similar issues, which can be surprisingly comforting. Knowing that others have walked the same path and come out smiling can be a huge relief.

When I was growing up, I was considered a "late bloomer." I was 16 years old. I thought something was wrong with me. I felt isolated and didn't talk to anyone about it, which just made it worse. I didn't realize I could talk to trusted adults about this or actively seek out friends who uplift me instead of being hurtful. For example, I didn't realize my aunt was an "early bird," taller than everyone in her class, and struggled with the same body image issues that I did, but for different reasons. My reason for telling you this is to reinforce that everyone's journey is their own, and there is nothing wrong with any of us! We are all completely normal on our own journey, and we must remember that every day.

Remember that puberty is just one part of your growth story, and it doesn't define who you are or who you will become. I'm not trying to scare you and make you dread this experience—I want to make sure I am setting you up for the possibilities of how things could go and who you can talk to about this. But whether you're an "early bird," a "late bloomer," or somewhere in the middle, you are moving at the pace that's right for you. Each person's body knows what it's doing, and trust me, it's doing its best for you. So, let's respect our bodies, support each other (always build others up), and recognize that whether "early" or "late," we all bloom beautifully at precisely the right time.

Your Body's Timetable: Understanding Your Unique Puberty Schedule

Think of puberty like a personal playlist—everyone has their unique mix of songs, and no two playlists are exactly the same. Just as you might enjoy a song that your friend doesn't, your body has its own way of changing and growing during puberty. Understanding and embracing your body's unique timetable is so important. Some of us might start noticing changes before others, while others might start seeing changes a bit later than others, and both are completely normal. What matters most is learning to move to your own rhythm and not comparing your growth to someone else's. Each body has its own internal clock, and it knows precisely what tempo to follow for changes like growth spurts or the start of menstruation.

Tracking your changes can be a fun and informative way to get tuned in with your body. Think about creating a personal growth chart or keeping a diary where you jot down changes you notice—anything from height increases to emotional shifts. This isn't just about noting physical changes; it's also about observing how you feel from day to day. Do certain changes make you excited? Nervous? Whatever your feelings, writing them down can help you process them more clearly and see how you evolve over time. This self-awareness builds confidence because you're actively engaging with your development, and it helps you see how far you've come.

Sometimes, you might have questions or feel unsure about the changes you're experiencing. This is completely normal! It's okay to seek guidance from trusted adults—be it parents, teachers, or healthcare providers. They can provide reassurance and clear up any confusion you might have. For instance, if you're wondering whether it's normal for one breast to be slightly larger than the other (it is!), asking a healthcare provider can give you peace of mind. Adults can share insights from their experiences and offer advice from a place of understanding and care. Remember, they've likely been through similar changes and can empathize with what you're going through. Nothing you are experiencing is unique in the world of puberty, so ask your questions because I guarantee that someone has been through it before.

Celebrating your milestones is a brilliant way to keep a positive outlook on puberty. Each new change can be seen as a personal victory, marking another step toward becoming the amazing young person you are meant to be. Got your period? That's a milestone! Noticed you're taller? That's another one! Even recognizing and managing your first mood swing is worth celebrating. These aren't just signs of getting older; they're clear indicators of your body's incredible ability to grow and adapt. So, cheer for yourself, throw a period party, or simply give yourself a pat on the back. Acknowledging and celebrating these milestones makes the process more fun and helps foster a healthy and positive self-image.

As you keep track of your puberty timeline, remember to stay patient and kind to yourself. Growth is a process, not a race. It unfolds differently for everyone, and that's what makes each of us unique. Whether you're the first among your friends to experience a certain change or the last, it doesn't define your worth or your journey. What matters is how you embrace your story with confidence and trust in the timing of your life. So, keep charting your growth, asking questions, and celebrating your milestones. Your body is doing exactly what it needs to do for you, and that, in every sense, is truly worth celebrating.

Pop Quiz

Let's play a little game to test some of the ideas we've talked about! This isn't just any quiz; it's a way to clear up some common misconceptions about puberty. Ready? Let's see how you do!

True or False: Everyone goes through puberty at the same time and in the same way.

False! Just like each of us has our own personality, each person's experience with puberty is unique. Some of us might start to notice changes as early as eight years old, while others might not see any changes until they're 14 or older. And that's completely normal. Even among friends or siblings, you might notice that everyone develops at different rates and in different ways. Some might grow taller first, while others might start developing breasts or get their period before seeing much height change. This variation is all part of how our bodies are programmed genetically, and other factors like nutrition and overall health play a role, too. So, if you find yourself comparing your puberty timeline to your friends', stop, catch yourself, and remember that puberty is not a race or a competition. Each body is on its own schedule, and that's perfectly okay.

True or False: If I ask a question to a trusted adult or parent, I will look stupid.

False! Asking questions is a fantastic way to learn and grow, and it's a sign of maturity and intelligence, not a weakness. Whether you're curious about the changes happening in your body, how to manage your emotions, or even how to handle other aspects of growing up, asking questions is a great way to get accurate information and support. Trusted adults—like parents, teachers, or even healthcare providers—usually appreciate your willingness to learn and are happy to help. They've been through similar experiences and can offer advice and reassurance based on knowledge and empathy. Remember, everyone had to learn about puberty at some point, and no one expects you to know everything. By asking questions, you're taking an active role in your growth and development, and that's something to be proud of.

True or False: My emotions, concerns, and experiences through puberty are unique, and no one could understand or help.

False! While your experiences during puberty are unique to you—like having your own personal twist on a common theme—many aspects of growing up are universal, and you're not alone in your feelings or experiences. It's normal to feel like no one understands what you're going through, especially when your emotions are all over the place. However, there are many people out there who can relate to and empathize with what you're feeling. Adults in your life, especially those you trust, can provide insights (maybe just a hug) and advice from their experiences. Opening up about your feelings and experiences allows others to offer support, guidance, and sometimes even solutions. Sharing your thoughts can help you feel less isolated and more supported. It's okay to ask for help and to talk about what you're going through. In fact, it's really brave.

So, how did you do on the quiz? Whether you got all the answers right or learned something new, I hope it helped reassure you about this natural part of growing up. Remember, puberty is a time of change and growth, both physically and emotionally, and it's filled with lots of questions and learning opportunities. Keep asking questions, seeking support, and, most importantly, being kind to yourself through all the changes. You're doing great, and you're not alone in this adventure. Feeling unsure about it all is completely normal!

TWO

Physical Changes

Imagine one day you wake up, and it feels like you've stepped into a whole new body—suddenly, things are starting to grow, change shape, and maybe even feel a bit awkward. That's kind of what going through puberty is like! It's like your body has hit the fast-forward button, and all these exciting and sometimes baffling changes are underway. In this chapter, we're diving into some of these physical changes, starting with one that many of you might be curious about or already noticing: breast development. Whether you're eagerly anticipating this change or feeling a bit anxious about it, I'm here to guide you through what to expect, how to handle some of the challenges, and how to embrace these changes with confidence and comfort.

Breast Development: What to Expect and When

Stages of Development

Breast development typically kicks off the whole puberty experience for many girls. It's one of the first signs that your body is starting on its path to becoming an adult. This change doesn't happen overnight, though—it's a gradual process that occurs in stages. These stages are medically categorized from I to V, starting from what your chest has always looked like as a kid (Stage I) all the way to fully matured breasts (Stage V).

In the early stages, you might notice a small, round bump beneath one or both nipples. This is a "breast bud," and it can be a bit tender when it first appears. Don't worry if one breast starts developing before the other; it's completely normal for breasts to grow at different rates. As you progress through these stages, your breasts will continue to grow and change shape, possibly becoming rounder and fuller. This growth typically spans several years, so giving your body the time it needs to develop at its own pace is crucial.

Variability of Growth

Now, let's talk about the variety of breast sizes and shapes because, just like faces, no two sets of breasts are exactly alike! Some might grow large, others might stay on the smaller side, and many will be somewhere in between. And yes, it's entirely normal for one breast to be slightly larger than the other. In fact, asymmetry is something many women experience, not just during puberty but throughout life. So, if you notice this in yourself, there's absolutely no need for concern. Remember, differences are completely normal, and they are all beautiful in their own unique way. The important thing is not how they look but that they are a healthy part of your body.

Dealing with Discomfort

As your breasts develop, you might feel some discomfort or tenderness, especially in the early stages. This is completely normal and usually nothing to worry about. Wearing soft, comfortable clothing can help ease this sensitivity. Some find that a soft, cotton sports bra or crop top provides the right amount of support and comfort during this time.

If the tenderness feels more pronounced and bothersome, chatting with your parents or guardians about what's best for you is a good idea. Also, gentle massages or warm compresses can soothe the soreness. Just remember, this discomfort won't last forever; it's just one part of the changes your body is going through.

Choosing the Right Bra

Finding the right bra can make a big difference in how comfortable you feel as your body changes. But with so many options out there, how do you choose? Well, the key is to look for something that feels good and provides the right level of support. Bras come in all shapes, sizes, and styles—from sports bras that keep everything secure when you're on the move to more structured styles that offer more shape and support.

When you're ready to start bra shopping, it might be helpful to go online with a trusted adult to look at all the styles and functionality to see what catches your eye. Here are a few bra types that you can look for to see if you like the style or functionality: bralette, demi, balconette, bandeau, t-shirt, convertible, push-up, sports, underwire, beginners, halter, racerback, or padded, to name a few. Maybe you are looking for a traditional bra with padding, underwire, lace, colors, etc. Or, maybe you want a style like a sports bra that allows greater movement if you are active but also feels more like an undershirt instead of that bra feeling. Maybe you need both styles!

Once you have an idea about your particular interests, it could be time to visit a store with knowledgeable staff who can help you find the right size and style or order a bunch of things online to try out at home and return what doesn't work.

You can also measure your bra size at home with a tape measure. Your first measurement will be around your chest, coming just under your breasts, and the second measurement will be around your chest, coming over your nipples. To come up with your cup size, you will subtract the 1st measurement from the 2nd. For example, your chest measurement just below the breast is 30" around. The chest measurement around the nipples is 31. The first measurement will be the bra size, and the second will be the cup size after subtracting. 31"—30" = 1", which translates into an A cup. (2" difference = B cup, 3" = C cup, etc.). So, in this case, your bra size is a 30A. This will give you an idea of where to start with sizing while shopping.

And remember, your bra size might change as you grow, so it's a good idea to get fitted more than once during puberty. There's quite a range compared to what was available even a decade ago, so don't settle—find one you like! Whether you prefer something plain and comfy or a bit fancier, there's a bra out there that's right for you.

As you navigate through all these changes, remember that this is your body, and it's doing exactly what it's supposed to do during this time. Every change is a step toward becoming the unique person you are meant to be. So take a deep breath, embrace the journey, and remember, you're not alone. Every girl goes through it, and plenty of support and guidance is available whenever you need it.

The Lowdown on Body Hair: Managing New Growth

As you navigate the bustling path of puberty, one of the changes you might start to notice is the appearance of new body hair. It's completely natural and another sign that your body is developing just as it should. Initially, you might find soft, fine hair in new places. Over time, this can become thicker and darker. This change typically begins under your arms, on your legs, and in the pubic area, which is completely normal and expected during puberty.

The pattern and timing of body hair growth can vary widely from person to person. Some might notice these changes quite early in puberty, while others might see them occur more gradually. Underarm hair usually starts to grow a couple of years after pubic hair begins to appear, and leg hair becomes more noticeable as both of these other areas continue to develop. It's important to remember that all these changes are part of how your body prepares for adulthood.

How we manage body hair is deeply personal and can be influenced by cultural or familial attitudes. In some cultures, body hair is barely noticed and often left as it grows. In others, there's a preference for removing it, which is done through various methods like shaving, waxing, or using hair removal creams. It's essential to know that how you handle your body hair is entirely up to you, and there's no right or wrong decision. If you decide to remove body hair, it's important to do so safely. For shaving, using a clean razor and shaving cream (I use Dove soap for sensitive skin) can help protect your skin from cuts and irritation. If you're considering waxing or creams, it might be helpful to talk with a trusted adult or a dermatologist to ensure it's done safely and to understand what's suitable for your skin type.

Taking care of your body as it changes includes good hygiene habits, which is especially important as your body begins to develop new hair. Regular bathing can help with any new body odors that arise during puberty and keep your skin clean and healthy. When it comes to body hair, washing the areas where hair grows thicker with mild soap (again, I use Dove soap for sensitive skin) and water is usually sufficient to keep your skin healthy. Remember, the goal of any hygiene routine is to make you feel comfortable and confident in your changing body.

Celebrating and accepting your body, including your body hair, is a wonderful form of self-love. Body positivity is all about accepting the changes your body goes through and recognizing the beauty in its natural state. Whether you remove body hair or let it grow, what matters most is how you feel about yourself. Each choice you make should support your comfort and confidence. Your body is your own, and loving it in every stage of its development is a powerful step toward embracing your true self. So, as you notice these new changes, remember that they are a normal part of growing up, and how you respond to them should align with what makes you feel best about yourself. It's easy to look around you and compare your journey to others, but I urge you to catch yourself, find a mirror, and remind yourself that you are perfect just the way you are.

Navigating Growth Spurts: Tips and Tales

Growth spurts during puberty are like your body's version of a sudden sprint in a long marathon—it's when you grow much faster than usual in a short amount of time. Typically kicking in two years after puberty starts, these spurts can see you shooting up several inches in height over just a few months! For girls, this rapid growth usually happens between the ages of 10 and 14. It's one of the most visible signs that puberty is in full swing, and it's also when you might suddenly find that your pants are too short or your shirtsleeves have crept up your arms overnight.

I was 14 when I had my growth spurt. I had no idea what was happening, but standing up made me dizzy! In the summer between 8th and 9th grade, I grew seven inches! Every morning, when I would get out of bed, I would feel dizzy when I stood up, and my mom couldn't keep up with my clothing needs. I still remember that feeling of dizziness, but the funny thing is I don't remember thinking, *Wow, I'm getting taller*—I just remember wondering why I felt dizzy every morning! It took me a minute (more like months) to equate this to my height.

So, adjusting to these rapid height changes can sometimes feel awkward. You might suddenly feel clumsier than usual. This is because your brain and muscles are trying to adapt to the new dimensions of your body. Imagine waking up one day and finding that your shoes are suddenly much longer or wider (go put on your dad or mom's shoes and walk around). It would take a bit of thought to walk, get to the door, and navigate the stairs! (My point is that you aren't on auto-pilot anymore with your movements.) That's similar to what your body is going through during a growth spurt. Simple tasks like gauging the distance to the next step on the stairs or timing your jump during sports might need a bit of recalibrating. My advice? Give yourself time to adjust. Be patient and keep a sense of humor about the occasional bumps and stumbles. Celebrate the bruises! They are just part of the process, and everyone going through puberty experiences them to some extent.

Finding clothes during growth spurts can also be a challenge. It might feel like you're constantly outgrowing everything! A good tip is to look for clothes with adjustable features (leggings are always a great go-to) or consider hemlines that can be let down. Belts, anyone? Also, opting for layers you can add or remove helps manage the body temperature changes that often come with growth spurts. Remember, everyone grows at their own pace, so try not to worry if your friends are buying new clothes for different reasons. What matters is finding comfortable outfits that make you feel good about yourself during this transforming phase.

The emotional adjustments during growth spurts are just as significant as the physical ones. When your body changes rapidly, it can feel like you don't even recognize yourself. This can stir up all sorts of feelings: excitement about looking more grown-up, frustration at the awkwardness, or even insecurity when you start standing out among your peers (like being taller than everyone else or being the first to show breasts). I want you to stand up tall and own your body in any state because when you are an adult, your body is also ever-changing, and how you manage this initial change will come with you for the rest of your life. You are beautiful!

It's also common to feel sensitive about comments from others regarding your height or appearance. Whether it's family teasing you affectionately about your new height or friends remarking on how different you look (my dad used to call me "chicken legs," *ugh*), what's important is how you internalize these comments. Try to view them as observations rather than judgments. Most comments are not meant to hurt you, but if they do, it's perfectly okay to let the person know you'd prefer not to focus on physical changes.

Overall, as a society, we are very focused on how we, and others, look. As a side effect, we associate the worthiness of ourselves and others based on pure vanity. As a result, we don't enjoy beauty—we compare ourselves to it. Therefore, most of our comments to ourselves and others (compliments or not) are focused on looks—"pretty," "ugly," "small" or "big." Social media plays a large role in this vanity, and we will talk about this more later in the book.

Challenge

Instead of telling someone they look pretty or nice, compliment the brain that puts that look together. For example, say, "I love those colors together" or "You have a great eye for fashion." And instead of looking at yourself in the mirror and judging how you look, take a step back and think about how you feel. Maybe you are just having an off day and feel putting on your favorite color will brighten you up a little, or maybe you are having a truly joyful day and feel black doesn't match the mood inside. How you feel is the most important thing, not how you look. We ALL look different, dress different, and feel different every day, and that's completely normal. You do you!

Building your confidence during this time involves embracing these changes positively. Handling these emotions involves being very kind to yourself and patient. Keep talking with the people you trust—sharing how you feel can make a big difference in how you cope—and believe me, you will feel so much better after you do. Talking things out can help you figure out your feelings and get you to where you feel good again. Surround yourself with friends and family who support you and make you feel good about yourself, no matter your height or size. And remember, every awkward moment is temporary and a place where laughter can always be found. You are evolving, and every change brings you closer to the adult you are becoming. Embrace these growth spurts with an open heart and a resilient spirit, and know that each change, each new inch of height, is a step toward the new heights you will reach in life.

Pop Quiz

Hey there! Ready to test your knowledge with a fun quiz? These questions are about celebrating your uniqueness and promoting a positive self-image during this time of change. Remember, there are no wrong answers here—this quiz is just a way to reflect on what you've learned and to think about your amazing journey in a fun, interactive way. Let's get started!

True or False: It's important to compare yourself to your friends to make sure you're on the right track with puberty.

False! Remember, puberty is a personal experience that happens at everyone's own pace. Comparing yourself to others can sometimes —most times—make you feel like you're not measuring up, but it's important to remember that everyone grows and changes at different times and in different ways. Your body knows what it's doing, and it's working hard to make all these changes at the right time for you. Celebrating your own milestones and embracing your body's unique timing are key to maintaining a positive self-image. So next time you find yourself comparing, try to shift your focus to all the wonderful things that make you, you!

True or False: Embracing your body's changes during puberty can boost your self-confidence.

True! Puberty is a time of significant change, and embracing these changes can help boost your self-confidence. Understanding and accepting the changes your body is going through can make you feel more in control and proud of what your body is capable of. Remember, each change is a step toward growing into the unique and amazing person you are, just on a bigger scale. By acknowledging and celebrating each new development, you're learning more about yourself and building a positive relationship with your body that will support your self-esteem.

Now that you've tackled these questions think about how each answer makes you feel about the changes you're experiencing. This quiz isn't just about right or wrong answers; it's about understanding more about yourself and learning to love all the parts of you that are growing and evolving. Keep these thoughts in mind as you navigate puberty with curiosity, confidence, and care for yourself.

THREE

Menstruation 101

Your First Period: What It Is and How to Prepare

Imagine you're about to embark on a grand adventure—a journey that every girl experiences, but each in her own unique way. Your first period marks a significant milestone in this adventure, and it's natural to feel a mix of excitement and nervousness. Think of this chapter as your trusty guidebook, equipping you with knowledge and tips to navigate this new terrain confidently.

Understanding Your Body's New Rhythms: Basic Anatomy and Menstruation

Let's start by getting familiar with the female reproductive system, which is incredibly smart and sophisticated—just like you. At its heart are two small but mighty organs called ovaries. Each month, these ovaries release an egg that travels through a tube called the fallopian tube toward the uterus, a cozy, muscular pouch in your lower belly. The walls of the uterus are lined with a special layer called the endometrium (big word, but the important part is to know that this lining is made up of blood, and this is what you "shed" every month). Here's where it gets interesting: your body prepares this lining each month for a fertilized egg, which would start a pregnancy.

If there's no fertilized egg, your body doesn't need the extra lining, and this is where menstruation comes in. It's your body's natural way of cleaning out this lining, which exits your body through the vagina. This flow is what we call your period. It's a natural, healthy process that happens to every girl and woman, and it plays a crucial role in the reproductive cycle.

Preparing for Your First Period

My Story: I got my first period when I was 16, and I truly wasn't prepared or had any information about it. One day, I came home from school, went to the bathroom, and noticed a brown, crusty substance in my underwear. I truly thought that I may have pooped my pants a little bit and didn't feel it! Seriously! So, of course, I didn't share that with anyone. Next day, same deal! I went to the bathroom after school and saw this brown, crusty substance again. Now I was getting really concerned. Somehow, I was pooping my pants without feeling it—this couldn't continue! So, this is when I looped my mom in. I showed her my underwear from the second day, and she immediately knew what it was. "You got your period!" she exclaimed. My mom was super excited, and I was in shock. I didn't feel any cramps and didn't feel anything coming out, and why was it brown? This wasn't what I thought my period would be like. All I had seen from the girls around me was "cramps," "pain," or not swimming at gym class. This was totally different (by the way, it was brown because that is the color of dried blood).

Now, knowing what's coming can make all the difference, so let's talk about how you can prepare and not have a panic moment where you think you are pooping your pants.

Managing Expectations: Flow, Duration, and Symptoms

Every period you have will present you with different symptoms, flow, and length, especially in the beginning. Gradually, you'll likely develop a more regular cycle, with periods lasting from three to seven days. Remember, every girl's body has its own schedule. Some might have a heavier flow, which might mean changing pads or tampons more frequently, while others might have a lighter flow.

Cramps are another part of periods for some girls. These are pains in your lower belly (closer to the area between your hips) caused by your uterus contracting (squeezing itself) to help shed its lining. If cramps bother you, gentle exercise (like a walk with your pet or parent), a warm bath, or a heating pad can help soothe them (I love my heating pad). It's also perfectly okay to talk to an adult about taking an over-the-counter pain reliever if the discomfort is too much. Personally, I have some periods where I feel no cramps and others when the heating pad is my new best friend for a few days.

Emotional Readiness: Embracing the Change with Confidence

Feeling confident about your first period comes with understanding what it is and knowing you're prepared. It's totally normal to feel a bit anxious or even excited about this change. These feelings are all part of growing up. Talking to someone who's been through it, like a mom, an aunt, or a teacher, can make you feel much more at ease. They can share their experiences and tips, and just knowing you have people to talk to can be a huge comfort. As I always tell my daughter, though, don't worry about what you can't control—just be prepared.

Respecting Privacy and Boundaries

As you start experiencing these changes, remember that your privacy matters. It's okay to choose who you talk to about your period. Some girls are open about it, while others prefer to keep it private, and that's perfectly fine. Your body, your rules. This is your personal experience, and you get to choose how to handle it. My younger sister told her friends for over a year that she had her period before she did, just so she would have an answer when asked about it. Some girls get excited about it and want to yell it from the rooftops. Again, this is a natural part of growing up, and, just like hairstyles, everyone experiences this differently and thinks about it differently. There is no wrong with the boundaries you set for yourself.

Choosing Period Products: A Guide to What's What

When it comes to managing your period flow, there's a whole world of products out there, each with its own set of benefits. It's like having a toolbox where every tool has a specific purpose; you just need to find the ones that work best for you. Let's walk through the different types of period products available to you, from the traditional to the innovative, and discuss how to choose the best options based on comfort, lifestyle, and personal values, especially when it comes to environmental impact.

Exploring the Variety of Period Products

First, let's talk about pads and tampons, which you might already be familiar with. Pads are often the go-to choice for many girls starting their periods. They are super easy to use. You simply stick them to your underwear, and they absorb the menstrual flow. They come in various sizes and thicknesses, which are typically labeled from light to heavy. This labeling helps you decide which pad to use based on how heavy your flow is at different times during your period. Some pads have wings that fold over the edges of your underwear to help hold them in place and prevent leaks, while others do not, which might be preferable if you find wings uncomfortable overall. It may feel weird at first to have this extra layer in your underwear, and you might think the whole world can see it bulging out of your pants! I promise this is not the case. You will be surprised by how discreet they actually are.

Tampons are another popular option. They are designed to be inserted into the vagina, where they absorb blood before it even leaves your body and hits your underwear. This can be especially handy for activities like swimming or sports where you might prefer not to wear a pad. Changing tampons regularly, about every four to eight hours, is important to maintain hygiene and health. The packaging will often help guide you on the right absorbency for your flow—using the lowest absorbency necessary for your flow helps reduce any risk of irritation or health issues like toxic shock syndrome (TSS), a rare but serious condition associated with tampon use. In the beginning, you may be using both a tampon and a pad until you can trust the products you are using and understand how they work for your body and flow.

Considering the Environment and New Innovations

In recent years, there's been a growing awareness of the environmental impact of period products. Traditional pads and tampons can contribute to landfill waste, as they are often made with plastic and other materials that aren't biodegradable. If you're thinking about the environment in your product choices, you might want to consider products like biodegradable pads and tampons or even reusable options like menstrual cups and period underwear. Let's go into detail about each of them.

Menstrual cups are made of medical-grade silicone and are designed to be inserted into the vagina to collect rather than absorb menstrual blood. Depending on your flow, they can be worn for up to 12 hours and then emptied, washed, and reused. Many find menstrual cups to be a cost-effective and eco-friendly alternative to pads and tampons, as they can last for several years with proper care. However, they can have a bit of a learning curve in terms of insertion and removal, so they might require some patience and practice initially. Once inserted, the tampon and the menstrual cup can't even be felt if inserted correctly.

Period underwear is another fantastic reusable option. These look and feel like regular underwear but have extra layers that absorb menstrual blood. They can be worn on their own or as a backup, along with tampons or a cup for extra protection. Like menstrual cups, period underwear is washable and reusable, making it another environmentally friendly option.

First-Time Use Tips: Learning the Ropes

If you're considering trying tampons or a menstrual cup for the first time, here are some tips to help make the experience a bit easier. For tampons, it's important to relax as much as possible. Tension can make insertion more difficult. Find a comfortable position, perhaps while sitting on the toilet or standing with one foot on the toilet seat, and use a tampon with an applicator, which can help guide it into the right spot. The insertion angle should be toward your lower back, not straight up.

For menstrual cups, the key is finding the fold that works best for you, as there are several ways to fold a cup for insertion. Like tampons, relaxing your muscles is important. Once inserted, give the cup a gentle turn to help create a suction seal, which prevents leaks. Removal involves gently pulling on the cup's stem to break the seal and then pulling it out. Remember, practice makes perfect, so don't get discouraged if it takes a few tries to feel comfortable.

Both the tampon and menstrual cup come with pictures on the packaging to help you through your first few times before you become a seasoned pro.

Embracing Reusable Options: Pads and Panties

Reusable pads function much like disposable ones but are made from materials that you can wash and wear again. They fasten to your underwear with snaps instead of adhesive and come in a variety of fabrics and absorbencies. Period panties can be worn without any other products on light days or as a backup on heavier days, providing peace of mind and reducing waste.

Choosing the right period products can feel overwhelming, but remember that it's all about what makes you feel comfortable and confident. Whether you prefer the convenience of disposables or are drawn to the sustainability of reusables, you have plenty of options to suit your needs and lifestyle. As you grow and your needs change, don't be afraid to try new products until you find your perfect match.

Disposal of a used tampon or pad is an important topic as well. I'm sure you've seen those signs in a public bathroom to "not flush down the toilet." This is true! You will usually see small bins on the walls of stalls in the public bathroom. You can place your used pad or tampon in these bins. If you are at home, you can wrap it up in a little toilet paper first before placing it in the garbage can (you can do this in the public restrooms as well). Do not flush these items down the toilet. If a pad or tampon is flushed down the toilet, it absorbs the water it is flushed with, grows in size, and usually clogs the pipes, sometimes with catastrophic results.

Period Kits for School: What to Include

Heading off to school when you're on your period can feel like a bit more of a challenge, but with a little preparation, it can be just as normal as any other day. Creating a period kit for school is like packing a mini survival bag—it has everything you need to handle your period discreetly and comfortably while you're away from home. Think of it as your secret toolbox that empowers you to tackle your school day head-on without worrying about your period catching you off guard.

Essentials for a Period Kit

Let's start with the basics. Your period kit should include a few sanitary items. Pads are a great starter choice because they're simple to use; just stick them in your underwear, and you're good to go. If you're using tampons, pack a few of those too. It's always good to have options depending on how you feel that day. Alongside these, throw in a spare pair of underwear. Accidents happen, and having a fresh set can be a game-changer in avoiding discomfort or embarrassment.

Now, even with the best protection, you might feel the need for a quick freshen-up. This is where wipes come in handy. They're perfect when you want to feel a bit cleaner but can't take a full shower. Choose unscented wipes to avoid irritation, and make sure they're flushable so you can dispose of them easily without harming the environment. All these essentials can be neatly packed in a discreet pouch or cosmetic bag. Opt for something compact yet cute—something that doesn't scream "period kit" so you can carry it around confidently without drawing any attention.

Hygiene Must-Haves

Maintaining good hygiene is super important during your period, especially when you're at school. Include a small bottle of hand sanitizer in your kit for those times when you can't get to a sink to wash your hands before and after changing your pad or tampon. Also, pack a few small, sealable bags—like those zip-lock bags used for snacks. They're perfect for discreetly disposing of used pads or tampons if you don't have immediate access to a trash can. This helps keep things hygienic and ensures you're respecting your environment and the people around you.

Putting together this period kit might seem like a small act, but it's a big step toward handling your periods with confidence, especially during school hours. It ensures you're prepared for anything the day throws at you, letting you focus on your classes, friends, and activities without stress. Remember, your period is a natural part of life, and with a little preparation, it doesn't have to disrupt your day or style.

Tracking Your Cycle: Why and How

Getting to know your menstrual cycle is like becoming fluent in the language your body speaks. It's not just about marking off days on a calendar; it's about connecting deeper with your body and understanding its rhythms and patterns. Why track your menstrual cycle, you ask? Well, for starters, it helps you predict when your period will start, which is super handy for planning sports, social events, or everyday activities. But more than that, tracking your cycle gives you insights into your overall health and moods, helping you recognize what's normal for your body and what might be a sign that you need to take extra care or consult a healthcare provider.

Getting to Know Your Cycle: More than Just Period Tracking

Most people think tracking your cycle just means marking the days you have your period, but there's so much more to it. Your menstrual cycle includes several phases, each affecting your body in different ways. By keeping track of these phases, you can learn a lot about your health and well-being. For instance, some girls find they feel more energetic on certain days of their cycle, while others might feel more tired or emotional just before their period starts.

The cycle starts with menstruation (remember, this is where your body sheds the lining in the uterus), but what follows is the "follicular phase," where hormones in your body prepare your body to release an egg. Then comes ovulation, the point in mid-cycle when the egg is released. After ovulation, there's the "luteal phase," where your body prepares for either pregnancy or the start of another cycle (menstruation). Tracking these phases and noting how you feel during each can give you incredible insights into how your body works, helping you make informed decisions about everything from exercise to emotional management.

How to Track Your Cycle: Tools and Tips

Now, how do you start tracking your cycle? Keep it simple with a calendar, a pen, or even a journal, which is totally fine and works great. Just mark the first day of your period and keep track of how long it lasts. But also, during the month, jot down if you woke up in a cranky mood, extra tired, or ready to take on the world! Also, jot down emotions from that day—maybe you were super happy all day, quick to cry, or just grumpy. Also, how did you sleep the night before? Were you really hungry that day? Maybe you weren't hungry at all, etc. Maybe your pants felt extra tight that day around your mid-section (some people call this "feeling bloated").

Keeping records like this is great at helping you spot and ultimately help predict how the different phases of your period will impact your overall emotions, mood swings, energy levels, cramps, sleep, and physical feelings. As your emotions are in full swing during this time in your life, these observations are important to keeping you in a good place. For example, if you wake up one morning just in a grumpy mood—but through your tracking, you also know that this phase of your period can make you feel that way—then you can work on being kinder to those around you and choosing words more carefully. So when your parent offers you a glass of orange juice for breakfast that morning, instead of saying, "No, I want grape juice!" you can catch yourself and say, "No, thank you. Do we have any grape juice?" Or if someone you care about catches that something might be off with you today, it's easier to say, "I'm just feeling a little grumpy today," and not accidentally take it out on someone else.

Respecting Your Privacy: Sharing Your Cycle Info

While tracking your cycle can be super helpful, it's also very personal. You might decide to share this info with a few people, like your doctor, a parent, or maybe a close friend, but it's totally up to you who you share this with, if anyone at all. Remember, this information is about your body and health, so who you share this with has to be what feels best for you.

Some girls find it helpful to share their tracking insights with a parent or trusted adult, especially if they're experiencing issues like an angry/sad/grumpy day, very painful cramps, or irregular periods, as these can sometimes need medical attention. But even then, how much you share and when is entirely your choice.

Tracking your menstrual cycle is a powerful way to take charge of your health and well-being. It helps you understand your body better, prepares you for each phase of your cycle, and can even clue you into your overall health. No matter how you choose to track it, the most important thing is that you're getting to know your body's patterns and rhythms. This knowledge empowers you to make informed decisions about your health and helps you develop a deeper connection with your body, celebrating its capabilities and understanding its signals.

Busting Period Myths

Let's clear the air about some common myths you might have heard about menstruation. It's super important to know what's true and what's not because believing myths can make you feel unnecessarily anxious or embarrassed about your period. So, grab your myth-busting gear, and let's set the record straight on some of the most popular misconceptions.

Addressing Common Myths: What's True and What's Not?

One of the biggest myths out there is that you can't go swimming during your period. This is totally false! Swimming during your period is absolutely fine. If you're worried about leakage, using a tampon or a menstrual cup can give you the protection you need to swim comfortably. These products are designed to be worn internally, collecting or absorbing your menstrual flow before it leaves your body, which means no worries about leaks. Just remember to change your tampon or empty your menstrual cup according to the instructions, usually every few hours, depending on your flow. This ensures you stay clean and comfortable while enjoying your swim. Plus, swimming can actually help ease period cramps by releasing endorphins, your body's natural painkillers, so it's a win-win situation!

Another myth that needs busting is the idea that period blood is dirty. This couldn't be further from the truth. Period blood is just a mixture of blood and tissue from your uterus lining, and it's as clean as any other blood in your body. The body is simply shedding what it doesn't need, and this process is a normal and healthy part of your reproductive cycle. So, there's nothing dirty or shameful about it—it's just another way your amazing body keeps itself in tip-top condition. But it looks like a brown color, you say? That is simply the color of drying blood, that's all.

Now, let's talk about the notion that everyone should have a 28-day menstrual cycle. In reality, menstrual cycles can vary a lot. While 28 days is often cited as the average, many people have shorter or longer cycles ranging anywhere from 21 to 35 days. What's important is what's regular for you. If your cycle falls consistently within this range and you're not experiencing any discomfort or irregularities that concern you, there's likely nothing to worry about. Your body has its own natural rhythm, and what's normal can differ from one person to another.

Do you live with other women, like your mom or sisters? If so, you might have heard that women who live together eventually end up with synchronized menstrual cycles. While it's a charming idea, there's actually no scientific evidence to support this. Menstrual synchrony is a myth that has been debunked by various studies. Each woman's cycle is influenced by her hormones, which aren't altered by those around her. So, while it might sometimes seem like you're all on the same schedule, it's just a coincidence.

And about the wild idea that having your period can attract bears or sharks if you're camping or swimming? This myth is definitely more suited to a dramatic movie scene than real life. There's no evidence suggesting that menstrual blood attracts more attention from wildlife than any other kind of human scent. Safety in natural habitats is always crucial, but your period isn't a special risk factor. So, whether you're on a fun camping trip or swimming in the ocean, your menstrual cycle doesn't put you at any more risk from wildlife than anyone else.

Understanding the truth behind these myths helps you manage your period with confidence and empowers you to make informed decisions about your health and activities. Menstruation is a natural, normal part of life, and nothing about it should keep you from enjoying your favorite activities or feeling good about your amazing body. So next time you hear a period myth, you'll know what to say!

Pop Quiz

Hey there! Ready for a little quiz fun? Let's play a game of True or False to shake off any myths and boost your confidence about menstruating. Remember, these questions are all about embracing positivity and humor while learning something new about your period. So, let's jump right in and see how well you can score!

True or False: Eating chocolate will make your period heavier.

False! While it might seem like a sweet remedy, eating chocolate doesn't directly affect the flow of your period. However, reaching for a piece of chocolate might actually help uplift your mood! Thanks to its feel-good ingredients, chocolate can be a comforting treat during your period. Just remember, moderation is key—too much of anything isn't great, even if it's as delicious as chocolate.

True or False: You should skip sports during your period.

False! There's no need to sit out gym class or skip your dance practice just because you're on your period. In fact, being active can actually help reduce symptoms like cramps and bloating. Exercise releases endorphins, which are your body's natural painkillers and mood lifters. So, lace up those sneakers and keep moving—your body will thank you!

True or False: Your period can turn the pool water red if you swim during it.

False! This is a classic myth and, let's be honest, sounds like a scene from a horror movie! When you're swimming, your menstrual flow slows down due to the water pressure, and if you're using a tampon or a menstrual cup, there's little chance of any leaks. So, dive in and enjoy the swim. Your period shouldn't stop you from making a splash and having fun in the pool!

True or False: You lose gallons of blood during each period.

False! It might feel like it, but during a typical period, a person only loses about three to five tablespoons of blood, on average. The amount can vary, but it's nowhere near gallons! Knowing this can help you keep any worries about blood loss in perspective. Your body is designed to handle this monthly process efficiently, so trust that it knows what it's doing.

Navigating your menstrual health is an important part of growing up, and understanding the facts can make you feel a lot more confident about your body's natural processes. Use this quiz as a stepping stone to embrace your period positively and with humor. Each correct answer is a win for breaking myths and spreading the truth!

FOUR

Personal Care and Hygiene

I magine you're embarking on an exciting expedition into the heart of a lush, vibrant jungle. Just as a seasoned explorer needs the right gear to navigate the wilderness, your body needs the right tools and knowledge to navigate the bustling growth and changes during puberty. In this chapter, we will discover how personal care and hygiene are about feeling confident and getting ready to take on the world!

Puberty and Hygiene: Keeping Clean and Confident

Changes in Hygiene Needs

As you step into puberty, your body starts to change gears and speed up in ways that might surprise you. One of the most noticeable changes is how your body begins to sweat more. This isn't just a random annoyance; it's your body's natural way of cooling down when it gets too hot. However, during puberty, hormonal changes kick your sweat glands into overdrive, leading to more sweat production than you might be used to. This increase in sweat can also start to mix with bacteria on the skin, which can produce a stronger body odor. It's completely normal, and everyone goes through it, but you might need to step up your hygiene game to keep feeling fresh and confident. Wahoo puberty!!...you get to be sweaty and stinky!

Causes of Body Odor

So, why does sweat smell more during puberty? It's all thanks to hormones! These chemical messengers, which become more active during your teenage years, stimulate your sweat glands to grow and produce different kinds of sweat. This sweat is richer in proteins and fats, which bacteria on your skin love to feed on. When bacteria break down this sweat, they produce that noticeable body odor. This process is completely natural and happens to everyone, although the intensity can vary from person to person.

Daily Hygiene Routine

Developing a daily hygiene routine is key to managing these new changes. Showering daily can help wash away sweat and reduce the bacteria on your skin that cause odors. It's especially important to wash areas where these sweat glands are abundant, like under your arms and around your groin. Use a mild, gentle soap to avoid irritating your skin, and make sure you dry off thoroughly afterward, as bacteria thrive in moist environments.

Adding deodorant to your morning routine can also make a big difference. Deodorants help mask the smell of body odor with a pleasant scent, while antiperspirants reduce sweating by temporarily blocking the pores that release sweat. If you're active in sports or sweat a lot, an antiperspirant might be a helpful choice. However, if you have sensitive skin or prefer not to interfere with your body's natural cooling system, a simple deodorant could be the way to go.

Choosing the Right Deodorant

When choosing a deodorant or antiperspirant, it's worth spending some time finding one that works well for your skin type and lifestyle. If you have sensitive skin, look for products labeled "hypoallergenic" or "for sensitive skin" to reduce the risk of skin irritation. There are also plenty of options out there free from aluminum and artificial fragrances, which can be gentler on your skin. Experiment with different types to see what feels best for you—sprays, sticks, roll-ons, or even creams. Each type has its benefits, and what matters most is that you feel comfortable and confident when using it. Talk to a trusted adult about what they use and why, and that may be a great place to start!

The Importance of Dental Hygiene

While it's easy to focus on body odor and sweat, let's not forget about taking care of your smile! Dental hygiene is super important during puberty, not just for keeping your teeth sparkling but also for overall health. Hormonal changes can make your gums more sensitive and susceptible to plaque and food particles, leading to more cavities if not properly cared for. Brushing your teeth at least twice a day with fluoride toothpaste, flossing daily, and using mouthwash can help keep your teeth and gums healthy. Regular check-ups with your dentist ensure that any potential issues are caught early, and professional cleanings can help keep tartar and plaque at bay.

Developing good hygiene habits now sets the stage for a lifetime of feeling good about yourself. It's all about caring for your body as it changes and grows, respecting and tuning into what it needs. By establishing these practices early on, you're not just warding off sweat and body odor or keeping your teeth clean; you're building confidence and learning to navigate your body's new landscape with grace and assurance. So embrace this time of transformation with open arms and a ready smile—you've got this!

Dealing with Acne: Skincare during Puberty

Imagine waking up to find a new pimple forming just when you thought your skin was clear. It can feel like your skin is out to get you sometimes, but really, it's just reacting to all the changes happening inside your body during puberty. Acne, one of the most common skin issues, often starts during these years due to hormonal changes. These hormones increase in both girls and boys during puberty and cause your skin's oil glands to enlarge and produce more sebum—an oily substance that can clog pores. This excess oil tends to mix with dead skin cells and sometimes bacteria on the surface of your skin, leading to unwelcome breakouts.

While it might seem like pimples pop up overnight, the process of forming acne can start weeks before you even see a blemish. Understanding this can help you realize why caring for your skin is so important, even when it looks clear. A simple but effective skincare routine can work wonders. Start with a gentle cleanser to wash away excess oil and impurities. It's best to wash your face twice a day, but if you find your skin getting too dry, using cleanser just in the evening is okay—just splash your face with water in the morning. After cleansing, use a light, oil-free moisturizer to hydrate your skin. Yes, even oily skin needs hydration! Over-drying can actually cause your skin to produce even more oil—as someone who has this kind of skin; I can completely understand why this makes no sense. However, moisturizing has saved me. And don't forget sunscreen in the morning! Not only is this a good practice to protect your skin as you get older, but many acne treatments can make your skin more sensitive to sunlight. Plus, protecting your skin from the sun helps prevent acne scars from darkening.

There are many skincare solutions out there that are affordable and available to you at your local grocery store! For example, perhaps start with just a cleanser and a moisturizer even before you experience any breakouts. If puberty is at your doorstep, this is not a bad habit to get into for the rest of your life. Talk to some adults in your life about their skincare routine to get some ideas on products and brands.

Now, despite your best efforts at home, sometimes acne can be stubborn, and it's okay to ask for help. If you're experiencing painful, deep, or very red pimples or if your acne is leaving scars, it might be time to see a dermatologist. These skin experts can offer treatments that aren't available over the counter and can tailor a plan specifically for your skin type and acne condition. Remember, everyone's skin is different, so what works for a friend might not work for you. A dermatologist can help you understand your unique skin needs.

Let's also clear up some myths about acne. It's a widespread belief that poor hygiene or certain foods, like chocolate or greasy snacks, can cause acne. However, acne is not a result of dirty skin, and while some individuals might notice certain foods seem to trigger their breakouts, these foods don't cause acne directly. It's more about how your body reacts to certain hormones and external factors. Stress can also impact acne, not because it directly causes pimples but because stress can prompt your body to produce more of the hormone that stimulates oil production. So, managing stress and maintaining a balanced lifestyle can be as important as your skincare routine.

By understanding what causes acne and how to care for your skin, you can feel more in control and less stressed when you spot a new pimple. A good skincare routine, paired with a healthy lifestyle and maybe some professional advice when needed, can help you keep your skin clear and your confidence up. Remember, acne is common during puberty and will usually become less of a problem as you get older. So, hang in there, and treat your skin with kindness—it's doing its best during these busy years of growth and change.

Hair Care: Managing Changes in Hair Texture and Volume

As you glide through the waves of puberty, you might notice that your hair begins to feel different, maybe curlier, straighter, thicker, or even thinner than before. These changes are completely normal and are another part of how your body evolves during this time. Just like the rest of you, your hair is responding to the hormonal symphony that's playing throughout puberty. These hormones can alter the texture and volume of your hair, making it seem like you're dealing with someone else's locks rather than your own! But don't worry—adapting your hair care routine can help you manage these changes and keep your hair looking fabulous.

When puberty hits, you might find that your hair suddenly feels oilier, or maybe it dries out and feels coarser. This is due to glands in your scalp reacting to hormonal fluctuations, which can increase their oil production. If your shiny, straight hair starts to wave or curl, it's because the follicles are responding to these inner changes, altering the shape and texture of your hair as it grows. Embracing these new changes with the right care routine is key to maintaining healthy, manageable hair.

Navigating through these changes starts with choosing the right shampoo and conditioner. The vast array of options might seem overwhelming, but focusing on your hair type and current needs can guide your choices. Just as with your skin care needs, there are plenty of affordable hair care options available to you, again, at the grocery store. What do the adults in your house use? That is a great place to start.

For oilier hair, look for shampoos labeled "volumizing" or "balancing," as they can help manage oil without stripping your hair of its natural moisture. If your hair has become drier, "hydrating" or "smoothing" products might be your new best friends, offering that extra moisture boost your locks crave. Remember, how often you wash your hair might change too. If oiliness is an issue, washing your hair every other day can help control it. However, if you're dealing with dryness, reducing your washes to two or three times a week can help preserve natural oils and prevent further drying.

For those days when washing isn't an option, or you need a quick fix, dry shampoo can be a lifesaver. A quick spritz at the roots can absorb excess oil, giving your hair a fresh look and more volume. Just be sure to use it sparingly, as too much can build up on your scalp and make your hair look dull. Another great tip for managing oily hair is experimenting with different hairstyles. Pulling your hair into a ponytail, braid, or fun updo can help manage the look of oiliness while giving you a stylish twist to your day-to-day look.

As your hair changes, it might also be the perfect time to experiment with new haircuts. A new style can help manage your hair's changing texture and boost your confidence. Layers, for example, can add volume and movement to hair that feels heavy or flat, while a shorter cut might be easier to manage if your hair has become thicker or curlier. Don't hesitate to consult a hairstylist—they can offer professional advice tailored to your hair type and help you find a cut that looks great and works well with your new hair texture.

Adapting to your hair's new needs during puberty doesn't have to be a chore or expensive. With some tweaks to your hair care routine and the courage to try new styles, you can embrace these changes confidently. Remember, your hair is a big part of how you express yourself, so have fun with it, experiment safely, and let your unique personality shine through every strand!

Hygiene for Private Areas: Caring for Your Changing Body

As we have discussed, puberty is causing your body to undergo numerous transformations, and staying attuned to these changes is key to your comfort and health. Among these changes, maintaining good hygiene for your private areas plays a crucial role. It's not just about feeling fresh and clean; it's about ensuring your delicate areas are well cared for to prevent discomfort and infections. Your body is a fine-tuned ecosystem, especially in areas as sensitive as your private ones, so knowing the right way to care for them can make all the difference.

Remember when you were little and while your mom or dad gave you a bath and cleaned your cute little baby bum, they would make a motorboat sound or say something silly like "cleaning your hiney" alongside a little tune? (Ok, well, that's what we did.) Anyway, somehow, when you are between baby and puberty, the bum (and the feet) seem to become a little less of a priority for some reason, but now, well, it's time to "clean the hiney" again!

First, let's talk about the importance of keeping your private area clean. This isn't about scrubbing more or using harsh soaps—it's about being gentle and attentive to what your body needs. The skin around your private parts is particularly sensitive, and during puberty, you might notice changes that require you to adjust your hygiene habits. For instance, you may start to experience more perspiration around this area, just like under your arms, or during particular times of menstruation, you may be painfully dry. This is completely normal, but it does mean that you might need to pay a bit more attention to keeping this area clean to feel comfortable and prevent any potential odor or infections.

Using the right products is essential for maintaining your private area's hygiene. Look for soaps and washes that are specifically designed for private areas—these are typically free from harsh chemicals and fragrances that can irritate your skin. Instead, they maintain the natural pH balance of your skin, which is crucial in keeping it healthy. For example, I use Dove soap for sensitive skin. Overwashing or using regular soap can disrupt this balance, leading to dryness or irritation. When you wash, do so gently and avoid scrubbing. Rinse thoroughly with warm water, and always pat the area dry with a clean towel to prevent moisture build-up, which can also lead to irritation.

Now, let's address a common concern: vaginal discharge. It might feel a bit weird (like you might feel like you just peed your pants a little) or even worrying when you first notice it, but vaginal discharge is a completely normal part of how your body keeps your intimate area clean and healthy. It helps to flush out cells and bacteria, keeping your vagina clean and preventing infections. The appearance and amount of discharge can vary throughout puberty and your menstrual cycle. Typically, it's clear or milky white and doesn't have a strong smell. However, if you notice changes in the color, smell, consistency (like it resembles oatmeal) or an amount of discharge that seems unusual—like if it turns yellow, green, itches, or has a strong odor—that is a good time to talk to a trusted adult or healthcare provider. They can help determine if it's just a normal part of your cycle or something that might need more attention.

Dispelling myths about private area hygiene is also important, as misinformation can lead you to do things that might do more harm than good. One common myth is that you need to use special products or douches to keep your vagina clean. In reality, the vagina is self-cleaning, and using these products may disrupt its natural environment, leading to irritation or infections. Another myth is that menstruation is unclean and that you should avoid bathing or washing your hair during your periods. This is entirely untrue.

Bathing during your periods is perfectly safe and helps you feel cleaner and more comfortable.

Understanding how to take care of your body as it changes is a vital part of growing up. By practicing good private area hygiene, you ensure that your body remains healthy and you feel comfortable and confident in your skin. Remember, each part of your body deserves care and respect, and knowing the right way to care for your private intimate area is a step toward loving and respecting your changing body. Keep these tips in mind, and don't hesitate to reach out to a trusted female adult or healthcare provider if you ever feel unsure about what's normal or need advice on private area care. Your body is your own, and taking care of it is a profound way to show love to yourself as you grow and navigate the many phases of your life. The adult females in your life have been through it all and probably tried it all, too—by opening that conversation with a trusted female adult, you will learn a lot and share a lot of giggles. I promise.

Pop Quiz

Hey there! Ready to have some fun while learning a bit more about your body during puberty? Today, we will explore some of the oddest, funniest truths about how our bodies change. Let's dive into this pop quiz with a pinch of humor and a lot of curiosity! Remember, these questions are just for laughs and learning—no need to worry about getting them all right!

True or False: Everyone must have a clear and smooth skin transition during puberty.

False! If there's one thing to know about puberty, it's that it can be a bit of a wild ride, and that includes your skin. Some might experience acne, while others might not, and both scenarios are completely normal. Hormonal changes can make your skin more oily, which sometimes leads to pimples or blackheads. If you're feeling self-conscious about acne, remember that many people go through this, and it doesn't last forever. What's most important is taking care of your skin by keeping it clean and finding a skincare routine that works for you. And remember, your worth isn't tied to how your skin looks. You are beautiful just the way you are, bumps and all!

Question 1: What do you call a sneaky body odor that seems to pop out of nowhere during class?

    A) A ninja whiff
    B) Surprise perfume
    C) A ghostly guest
    D) Homework stress scent

While it might feel like a ghostly guest, the correct answer is A) A ninja whiff! Yep, sometimes body odors sneak up on us during the least convenient times, like right in the middle of class. This happens because, during puberty, your body starts producing more sweat due to the increased activity of sweat glands. The interaction between the sweat and natural bacteria on your skin can lead to new, sometimes surprising scents. But no worries, a little deodorant, and regular showers can usually keep these ninja whiffs at bay.

Question 2: If your body odors were a Taylor Swift song, what would their hit single be called?

    A) "Better than Revenge"
    B) "Breathless"
    C) "Sweet Nothing"
    D) "This Is Why We Can't Have Nice Things"

While all these titles might hit the Billboard charts in the world of scents, the winner here is B) "Breathless." It's a playful nod to the fact that during puberty, body odors can leave you feeling breathless, and you probably think those around you feel the same way! Hormones are the main conductors of this funky symphony, leading to increased sweat production. Managing your personal scent playlist might require trial and error with different hygiene products, but you'll soon find the right rhythm to keep those odors in harmony.

Question 3: How would you describe the moment you realized you needed to step up your foot hygiene game?

> A) Like discovering a forgotten science project in your basement
> B) Realizing your sneakers have started a band, and it's not music to your ears
> C) Like walking into a mystery that needs solving
> D) All of the above

The best answer? D) All of the above. Discovering that your feet can produce such a robust aroma can be quite the science project gone wrong! Like any good detective, solving the case of the smelly sneakers involves some investigation and action. Thanks to all those hormonal changes, the feet can get extra sweaty and smelly during puberty. Wearing breathable socks, choosing the right footwear, and maintaining good foot hygiene can help clear up this mystery and keep your feet feeling fresh. A popular sign that you may need to step up the foot hygiene game is that when you take your shoes off, your grandma's nose wrinkles on the other side of the room, and she asks, "What's that smell?"

Quiz Wrap-Up

Great job on tackling those questions! Whether you guessed right or just had a good laugh, remember that experiencing new and sometimes strange body odors during puberty is completely normal. It's all part of growing up, and with the right tools—like deodorant, daily showers, and a sense of humor—you can handle anything your body throws your way. Keep smiling, keep learning, and remember, every quirky part of puberty is just another note in the unique melody that is you!

FIVE

Healthy Lifestyle Choices

Imagine you're the artist of your own life's mural, mixing and blending colors to create a masterpiece. Just as an artist needs the right colors to express themselves, you need the right blend of foods to nourish your body, especially during the colorful phase of puberty. This chapter is like your color choices, filled with vibrant tips and essential knowledge to help you paint a healthy, joyful, and balanced life.

Mindful Eating: Nutrition and Puberty

Balancing Your Diet during Puberty: Why It Matters

I know, I know, we are talking about diet. But believe me, I'm not talking about going ON a diet—I'm talking about giving your body the fuel it needs as you grow. As you step into puberty, your body becomes a busy construction site, building bones, growing muscles, and undergoing many other changes that require plenty of nutrients. Think of these nutrients as the building blocks and tools needed on this site. A balanced diet (again, not going on a diet) ensures that your body has a steady supply of these essential materials at a time when it's constructing the adult version of you. This doesn't mean focusing solely on calories but rather on the quality and variety of foods you eat, ensuring you get a rich mix of the nutrients necessary to support your rapid growth and development.

Imagine your plate as a colorful garden, where each part provides a different nutrient your body needs. Vegetables and fruits add vitamins and minerals essential for your immune system and overall health. Proteins from meat, beans, or nuts are like bricks laying down muscle and cell structure. Carbohydrates from grains and potatoes are the energy currency to fuel all your activities, from schoolwork to sports. And don't forget dairy or its alternatives, which are rich in calcium and crucial for building strong bones that will support your body like the sturdy frame of a house. Colorful is the word here: Make your plate as colorful as possible, and you will be much closer to getting the nutrients you need.

To give you an example of what this could look like:

- **Breakfast**: Apple slices, milk, bacon, eggs with cheese, and water
- **Lunch/Snack**: Apple slices, water, carrots, and leftovers from last night's dinner, perhaps?
- **Dinner:** Meat (or substitute for that protein), vegetable (roasted broccoli and cauliflower with parmesan cheese is my favorite), water, and a starch (potato or brown rice)

And of course, if you've eaten a delicious dinner like that, dessert must follow. Everything in moderation matters, and that's why I don't give a dessert recommendation. After that dinner, enjoy your favorite dessert.

Mindful Eating: Listening to Your Body

Mindful eating is about creating a healthy relationship with food by paying attention to how it affects your body and mind. It means eating with intention and attention, noticing how different foods make you feel, and how your body cues hunger and fullness. Listen to your body—it's smart! When you're really hungry, your body asks for fuel (not chips). When you feel full, it's telling you it has what it needs. Eating should be a response to these internal cues, not just external ones like time of day or what others around you are doing.

Here's a fun way to practice mindful eating: Next time you have a meal, try focusing on the flavors, textures, and smells. Enjoy each bite and chew slowly. This helps with digestion and allows you to check in with your body's hunger signals. Did you know it takes about 20 minutes for your brain to register fullness? 20 minutes! Eating slowly gives you time to recognize when you're full, which can help prevent overeating.

Nutrient-Rich Foods: Your Body's Best Friends

During puberty, certain nutrients are superstars when it comes to your health. Calcium, for example, is essential for developing strong bones, which is crucial as you're reaching your peak bone-building years. Good sources of calcium include dairy products like milk and cheese, as well as plant-based options like broccoli, kale, and fortified almond or soy milk.

Iron is another key nutrient, especially for girls, as it helps make new blood cells and carry oxygen in your body. With the onset of menstruation, getting enough iron becomes crucial to prevent anemia, a condition that can make you feel tired and weak. Lean meats, spinach, and iron-fortified cereals are great sources. Pairing iron-rich foods with those high in vitamin C, like oranges or bell peppers, can help your body absorb iron more effectively.

I also want to point out here that you desiring new, or better, foods in your household will usually be a welcome change for the adults in your life. Modern lifestyles are busy, and doing our best to get food in our bellies sometimes leads to foods laced with sugar, sodium, and unhealthy carbohydrates. What's an unhealthy carbohydrate, you ask (because you've probably only heard that carbs are bad, right)? Carbs are not bad—they are essential for activity, but there is such a thing as good and bad carbs. A bad carb is any carbohydrate that has added sugar is an unhealthy carb. Period, it's that simple.

Nurturing a Healthy Food Relationship

Maintaining a healthy relationship with food means recognizing that eating nourishes your body and soul. It's perfectly okay to enjoy a cookie or a piece of cake; these foods can be part of a balanced diet. The key is moderation, not labeling foods as "good" or "bad." If you ever feel anxious about food or your body image, talking to someone you trust is important. Whether it's a parent, a teacher, or a counselor, they can provide support and knowledge or help you find the resources you might need.

Debunking Diet Myths: Embracing Food Facts

Let's clear up some common food myths! One popular myth is that skipping meals can help you manage your weight. In reality, missing meals can make you hungrier, and you might end up eating more later. The only way to burn fat is by having muscle. If you skip meals, you lose muscle before losing any fat. Another myth is that carbs are bad. Carbohydrates are actually the primary energy source for your body, especially your brain. Instead of cutting them out, choose whole grains like brown rice or whole wheat bread, which provide energy, valuable nutrients, and fiber. If you are worried about "fat" (which is a biological makeup of every human's body), remember that muscle is the only thing that burns fat. Skipping meals doesn't burn fat, it burns muscle.

Promoting Body Positivity: Beyond the Scale

Finally, embracing body positivity means appreciating your body for what it can do rather than focusing on what it looks like or what the scale says (FYI, more muscle = higher weight). Your body is an incredible instrument, not an ornament. It allows you to experience the world, play sports, dance, laugh, give hugs, and love. Treat it with kindness and respect, feeding it nourishing foods not just to look a certain way but to live fully and healthily. Remember, true beauty blooms from within—a healthy, happy body and a fulfilled heart are where real fulfillment lies.

Embracing these principles of mindful eating and balanced nutrition can help you navigate puberty with energy, vitality, and confidence. By understanding and nurturing your body's needs, you're setting the stage for a healthy life rich in experiences and joy.

The Power of Exercise: Finding Fun in Activities You Love

Discovering the Joy and Benefits of Regular Exercise

When we think about exercise, it's easy to picture hard workouts that leave you breathless, but exercise is so much more—it's any movement that gets your heart rate up and brings a bit of sweat. During puberty, when your body and emotions are riding a roller coaster, engaging in regular physical activity can be a fantastic way to smooth out the ups and downs. Physically, it helps build stronger bones and muscles, boosts your stamina, and can improve your skin health by increasing blood flow, which helps to clear toxins from your body. But the benefits aren't just physical; they extend to your mental and emotional well-being, too.

Exercise acts like a natural mood lifter. Have you ever noticed how you feel more relaxed and happier after some active play outside or a dance session in your room? That's because being active releases endorphins, sometimes called "happiness hormones," which have the power to improve your mood and decrease feelings of stress and anxiety. Especially during puberty, when mood swings can suddenly turn your day upside down, a quick jump rope session or a brisk walk with your dog can bring back some balance and make things feel a bit brighter. I personally always find it amazing after I've done a workout or gotten out into nature how much calmer I feel about everything—like I can take anything on at that point. For me, two days of no activity = Grumpy Gus.

Moreover, regular activity helps you sleep better by helping your body wind down and relax at night. And good sleep is crucial during these years when your body is getting its factory settings updated for adulthood. So, not only does exercise help you feel more upbeat and energetic during the day, but it also helps you catch those much-needed Z's at night, ensuring you wake up refreshed and ready to tackle whatever comes your way. More importantly, keeping a regular sleep schedule every day of the week is so important. But you're thinking, *It's Friday night! Why can't I stay up later? I don't have to get up in the morning!* Well, did you ever notice that even on the weekends, your body tends to wake up at the same time you wake up on a school day? That's because your body is on a schedule. The more you keep it on this schedule, the better off your body will be while building your big brain and your bigger body.

Exploring a World of Activities: Find What Makes You Move

Finding the type of exercise you love can turn a "must-do" task into a "want-to-do" joy! Not everyone is into team sports or running, and that's totally okay. The key is to try different activities to discover what clicks for you. Maybe it's swimming, where you can feel weightless and swift. Or perhaps it's martial arts, where you can learn cool moves and self-discipline at the same time. Ever thought about rock climbing? It's great for your body and boosts your problem-solving skills as you find the best route to the top. What about a trampoline park or ninja gym that offers an unlimited play option? Or perhaps just going for a walk with the dog—you do you!

Also, consider activities like dancing, hiking, or even yoga, which improve your flexibility and balance and help you learn to breathe deeply and calm your mind. The options are endless, and the best part is that you can switch things up whenever you want. The goal is to make moving your body a fun and regular part of your day. Invite friends to join you, or take this time to have some moments to yourself, reconnecting with your thoughts and feelings through movement.

Boosting Self-Esteem Through Strength and Capability

Regular physical activity is a fantastic way to boost your self-esteem. Every time you meet a small goal, overcome a challenge, or simply stick to your exercise routine, you're building muscle and confidence. You're proving to yourself that you can set goals and achieve them, rely on your body, and push through even when it gets tough. This kind of confidence spills over into other areas of your life, helping you feel more capable and self-assured whether you're answering a question in class, standing up for a friend, or trying out for the school play.

So, consider exercise a celebration of what your body can do, and find activities that make you feel excited, strong, and alive. Remember, every bit of movement counts, and the most important thing is that you enjoy it. By integrating physical activity into your life now, you're setting up habits that will keep you healthy, happy, and glowing with confidence for years to come. Here's to finding your movement joy and reveling in every jump, kick, and dance step along the way!

Stress Reduction Techniques for Tweens

Understanding What Stresses You Out

Let's be real for a second—puberty can be like riding a super fast roller coaster. It's thrilling but also can get pretty overwhelming. During this time, you might face several stressors that weren't much of a concern before. Schoolwork, for instance, often gets more challenging as you move into higher grades, with more homework and tougher subjects. Then there are the social dynamics—friendships can shift, and social circles can change, sometimes daily. And let's not overlook the physical changes your body is going through, which can be a source of anxiety and confusion by themselves.

Recognizing these common stress triggers is the first step in managing them. It's like being a detective in your own life—the better you understand what causes your stress, the more effectively you can address it. Sometimes, just naming these pressures can make them feel less daunting. Try keeping a journal where you can note when you feel stressed and what seems to trigger it. You might start to see patterns, like maybe you feel more anxious when you have a math test or when there's a big social event (which is completely normal, by the way—pretty much everyone feels that way). Once you know your stressors, you're better equipped to tackle them head-on.

Simple Yet Powerful Stress Busters

Now, onto some good news—there are lots of simple and effective ways to reduce stress, and they don't require anything fancy. Deep breathing, for example, is something you can do anywhere, anytime. It's all about taking slow, deep breaths to help calm your mind and body. Imagine your breath as a wave: as you breathe in, the wave rises, and as you breathe out, it gently falls. This can help slow down a racing heart and bring peace to your busy mind.

Journaling is more than just keeping a diary. It's a way to express your feelings and unload some thoughts that might be crowding your mind. You can write about your day, doodle, or even make lists of things you're grateful for. Seeing your thoughts on paper can make them easier to manage and give you a new perspective on what's bothering you.

The Joy of Doing Nothing: The Art of Downtime

In a world that often celebrates being busy all the time, it's important to remember the value of doing nothing. Yes, you heard that right—sometimes, the best thing you can do for yourself is just chill. Downtime is not wasted time; your brain needs to relax and recharge. The quiet moments, like reading a book, listening to music, or just daydreaming, can be the most refreshing. Downtime does not include scrolling on a phone. Downtime is a screen-free time period. I know I just said something that made you raise your eyebrows because usually every human around you is on their phone all the time, downtime or not. I am challenging you and your generation to change this—use your brain to stay creative and away from technology for as long as you can.

Make sure to schedule time into your day just to do things that make you happy and relaxed. Whether crafting, playing with your pet, gardening, or going for a walk, these activities are not just fun

—they're necessary for your mental health. They help you unwind and connect with what brings you joy, keeping stress at bay.

When to Seek More Support

Sometimes, despite your best efforts, stress can feel overwhelming, and that's perfectly okay. It's important to know when to ask for help. If you ever feel like your stress is too much to handle on your own or it's affecting how you eat, sleep, or interact with others, it might be time to reach out.

Talking to trusted adults can be a huge relief. Whether it's a parent, teacher, or coach, these people care about you and can offer support and advice. Sometimes, just talking about what's bothering you can make a big difference. I hope that's been the tone of this entire book so far, though. This experience of puberty is not unique to you, and talking to a trusted adult (who understands what is going on for you at this time) will make all the difference in the world...over and over again. Puberty, emotions, and stress are not unique, nor should they be isolating.

Remember, everyone experiences stress—it's a normal part of life. But with the right tools and support, you can manage it effectively and keep it from overwhelming you. By learning to recognize your stressors, using simple techniques to keep stress at bay, enjoying downtime, and seeking help when needed, you're well on your way to surviving and thriving during these exciting, transformative years.

Getting Enough Sleep: Tips for Restful Nights

The Essential Role of Sleep during Your Growing Years

I know we have touched on this already, but this is so important. For a kid, you've been told to get to bed early your entire life, and now you are waiting for that 10 pm bedtime as you get older. When you are an adult, you can choose your bedtime, but right now, your body and brain require more sleep than at any other time in your life. Whether that's "cool" or not, those are the facts. Respect your body and take care of yourself to be the best adult you can be.

Navigating through puberty is no small feat—your body and mind are in a constant state of growth and adjustment. Amidst all these changes, sleep becomes not just a restful break but a critical ally. During those quiet hours of sleep, your body does some of its most important work. Growth hormones are most actively released while you're sleeping, aiding in everything from increasing your height to strengthening your bones. Moreover, as your brain recharges during a good night's rest, it processes and consolidates all the new information you've encountered during the day, helping with memory and learning. Emotionally, sleep is a reset button; it helps regulate moods and manage stress, making those emotional ups and downs of puberty a bit easier to handle.

But let's get practical—how can you ensure you're getting all the sleep your body desperately needs during this hectic phase of life? Setting up a sleep-conducive environment is a great start. Begin by looking at your bedroom through the lens of comfort and tranquility. A cool, dark, and quiet room often makes for the ideal sleep environment. Consider blackout curtains if street lights peek through your windows or a fan or white noise machine if there's noise you can't control. And what about your mattress and pillows? They should support your body comfortably, making you feel like you're sleeping on clouds.

Another crucial element in your sleep environment is the presence, or rather the absence, of screens. The blue light emitted by phones, tablets, computers, and TVs can seriously mess with your ability to fall asleep. It tricks your brain into thinking it's still daytime, reducing the production of melatonin, the hormone that makes you sleepy. Try to turn off all screens at least an hour before bed. Wind down with a book, some gentle stretches, or a soothing music playlist. This helps your mind relax and signals to your body that it's time to power down.

Navigating Common Sleep Challenges

As simple as it sounds to get enough sleep, many tweens find themselves tossing and turning at night, struggling with common sleep challenges like insomnia or finding it hard to wake up in the morning. If you find yourself staring at the ceiling long after you've hit the bed or if morning alarms feel like your worst enemy, know that you're not alone. Many of these issues stem from the natural shifts in your internal clock during puberty, often pushing you to feel more awake late at night and making mornings feel impossibly early.

One effective strategy to combat these challenges is establishing a consistent bedtime routine. This doesn't mean just going to bed at the same time every night, though that's a great start. It's about creating a series of relaxing activities leading up to bedtime, signaling to your body it's time to slow down. Maybe it's a warm shower, followed by some light reading or journaling. Keeping this routine even on weekends can help regulate your sleep cycle, making sleep more restful and mornings less groggy.

For those nights when sleep just won't come, instead of lying in bed growing more frustrated by the minute, try getting up and doing something calm and soothing in low light. This could be something like coloring, knitting, reading an actual book (not Kindle), or putting together a puzzle. Once you feel sleepy, go back to bed. Sometimes, just breaking the cycle of lying in bed worrying about not sleeping is enough to reset your mind and body.

Adapting to Your Changing Sleep Needs

Understanding that your sleep needs to evolve as you grow is key. During puberty, your body might need more sleep than before—experts recommend 8 to 10 hours each night for tweens and teens. However, with school, homework, sports, and maybe even social commitments, squeezing in those hours can sometimes feel like a puzzle. Prioritizing sleep is crucial; think of it as charging your body's battery. Without enough charge, everything from your school performance to your mood and health can be impacted.

Setting a regular bedtime and a wake-up time that allows for those 8 to 10 hours of sleep is a good practice. It might mean rearranging some of your evening or morning activities, but your body will thank you for it. If you're finding it hard to meet your sleep needs during the week, try not to overcompensate by sleeping in too long on weekends, which can throw off your sleep cycle come Monday. A nap during the day can be a good way to catch up on missed sleep, but keep it to about 20 to 30 minutes; longer naps can make it harder to fall asleep at night.

Sleep and Your Emotional Well-being

Never underestimate the power of sleep on your mood. It's amazing how much more manageable the world can seem after a good night's sleep. A good night's sleep helps you handle stress, manage your emotions, and face challenges with a clearer head. On the flip side, lack of sleep can make everything feel more intense and overwhelming. If you ever find yourself feeling unusually anxious, irritable, or down, it might be worth looking at your sleep habits. Are you getting enough rest? Is your sleep quality good? Sometimes, making small adjustments to your sleep can have a big impact on your emotions.

Pop Quiz

Hey, ready for a little quiz fun that's all about you and how you're managing your sleep, exercise, and personal regulation during these exciting times of change? These questions are designed to be a cozy checkpoint to see how well you're tuning into your body's needs and taking care of yourself. No pressure—it's just a cool way to reflect on what you've learned and maybe even discover new things about yourself! Let's get started:

Question 1: What's a great way to ensure you're getting enough exercise every week?

A) Stick to exactly the same routine daily.
B) Mix different types of activities you enjoy throughout the week.
C) Only focus on weekend sports.
D) Exercise only when you have extra energy.

Correct Answer: A) Stick to exactly the same routine daily. OR B) Mix different types of activities you enjoy throughout the week. These are both the right answers, depending on your lifestyle. Putting a routine together could help keep you on track; however, if a routine just won't cut your schedule, keeping your exercise routine varied and fun can help you stick to it. Whether dancing in your room, playing a sport, or going for walks, doing activities you love makes it much easier to keep moving. Plus, mixing it up can help all parts of your body get a good workout and keep you from getting bored.

Question 2: What's a smart strategy to help you wind down before bedtime for a restful night's sleep?

    A) Scroll through social media until you feel tired.
    B) Drink a big cup of coffee and hope for the best.
    C) Create a calming bedtime routine, like reading or listening to soft music.
    D) Tackle your homework right before bed to keep your mind busy.

Correct Answer: C) Create a calming bedtime routine, like reading (an actual book, not Kindle) or listening to soft music. Establishing a relaxing routine before bed can significantly improve your sleep quality. Activities that calm your mind, like reading a book or listening to gentle music, signal to your body that it's time to slow down and prepare for sleep, helping you drift off more easily.

Question 3: If your friend is feeling stressed and overwhelmed, what's a good piece of advice you could offer?

    A) Ignore the stress; it'll probably go away on its own.
    B) Suggest they try some relaxation techniques like deep breathing or meditation.
    C) Recommend they stay up all night worrying about it.
    D) Tell them to take on more activities to keep their mind off stress.

Correct Answer: B) Suggest they try relaxation techniques like deep breathing. Stress can be managed effectively with simple relaxation techniques. Encouraging your friend to take a few deep breaths can help them feel more in control and less overwhelmed. It's also a great way for you to help your friends by sharing healthy coping strategies!

Question 4: Why is it important to listen to your body's signals, like feeling tired or full?

> A) Ignoring your body's signals is a good strategy to build endurance.
> B) Your body doesn't actually know what it needs.
> C) It helps you take better care of yourself by meeting your physical and emotional needs.
> D) It's not really important; just push through no matter what.

Correct Answer: C) It helps you take better care of yourself by meeting your physical and emotional needs. Listening to what your body is telling you, like when you need rest or when you're full, is key to self-care. It ensures you're addressing your physical needs and respecting your body's limits, which is essential for overall health and well-being.

Wow, you did it! How did you do? Remember, this quiz isn't just about right answers—it's about thinking through your daily habits and maybe even improving them. Each question is a little nudge to remind you that taking care of your body and mind is super important and totally within your control. So keep listening to your body, enjoying activities that make you smile, and ensuring you get that precious sleep. You're doing great, and every small step you take is helping you grow into your best self!

Make a Difference with Your Review
UNLOCK THE POWER OF GENEROSITY

"Kindness is the language which the deaf can hear and the blind can see."

Mark Twain

People who give without expecting anything in return live happier lives. So if we have a chance to do that together, let's go for it!

To make that happen, I have a question for you…

Would you help someone you've never met, even if you never got credit for it?

Who is this person, you ask? They are like you. Or, at least, like you used to be. Less experienced, wanting to make a difference, and needing help, but not sure where to look.

Our mission is to make understanding social media's influence on young girls and puberty accessible to everyone. Everything we do stems from that mission. And the only way for us to accomplish that mission is by reaching…well…everyone.

This is where you come in. Most people do, in fact, judge a book by its cover (and its reviews). So here's my ask on behalf of a struggling young girl or her parent/guardian you've never met:

Please help that young girl or parent/guardian by leaving this book a review.

Your gift costs no money and less than 60 seconds to make real, but can change a fellow young girl's or parent/guardian's life forever. Your review could help…

- One more girl not be impacted by cyberbullying.
- One more girl understand her worth is not on her phone.
- One more parent understand how important their role is.
- One more girl feel empowered to put down her phone.
- One more dream come true.

To get that 'feel good' feeling and help this person for real, all you have to do is...and it takes less than 60 seconds...leave a review.

Simply scan the QR code below to leave your review:

If you feel good about helping a faceless young girl or her parent/guardian, you are my kind of person. Welcome to the club. You're one of us.

I'm that much more excited to help you navigate your own puberty journey faster than you can possibly imagine. You'll love the strategies I'm about to share in the coming chapters.

Thank you from the bottom of my heart. Now, back to our regularly scheduled program.

Your biggest fan,

Kim Cranston

PS - Fun fact: If you provide something of value to another person, it makes you more valuable to them. If you'd like goodwill straight from another young girl or their parent/guardian - and you believe this book will help them - send this book their way.

SIX

Emotional Rollercoaster

Imagine you're on a stage, spotlight shining down, about to deliver the performance of a lifetime, and suddenly your emotions are the audience, each one reacting differently—some cheer, some boo, and some sit quietly. This is a bit like going through puberty; it's a performance where your emotions can change unexpectedly, leaving you feeling like you're in a spotlight trying to understand the crowd's reaction. This chapter, dear reader, is your backstage pass to understanding and managing the whirlwind of emotions that come with puberty. Let's step behind the curtain and learn how to navigate this emotive journey with grace and confidence.

Feeling All the Feels: Navigating Emotions during Puberty

Understanding Emotional Fluctuations

First things first: the emotional rollercoaster you're on is powered by hormones. That fact alone is a reason to show yourself and others some grace. These little chemical messengers are like the directors of your puberty play, influencing not just how your body changes but also how you feel. As your body begins to produce more hormones like estrogen and testosterone, you might feel one way this minute and completely different the next. This is completely normal. Hormones can affect neurotransmitters in your brain—the chemicals that send messages about how you're feeling. So, if sometimes it seems like your emotions are riding a fast-moving carousel, it's because, in a way, they are.

It's important to remember that every girl experiences these changes, though the specifics can vary. Some might feel more irritable or moody, while others might feel anxious or overly sensitive. And sometimes, you might even feel all these things in the course of one day! While it can be bewildering, understanding that these fluctuations are a normal part of growing up can help you feel more grounded. Just like knowing the rules of a game makes playing it easier, understanding what's happening inside you makes navigating these changes less daunting.

Identifying Emotions

Now, let's talk about tuning into your emotional world. Being able to recognize and name what you're feeling is like having a map in this new territory. Start by paying attention to physical clues. For instance, does your stomach twist into knots when you're nervous? Does your heart race when you're excited? Noticing these signs can help you connect physical reactions to emotional states.

Keeping an emotion journal can be incredibly helpful. Each day, jot down a few notes about how you felt at different times and what was happening around you. This not only helps in identifying patterns but also makes your feelings more tangible and manageable. Sometimes, just writing down that you feel sad, angry, or happy can take some of the power out of the emotion and help you understand it better.

Healthy Expression

Expressing your emotions is as important as understanding them. Bottling up feelings usually makes them harder to handle in the long run. So, how can you express what you're feeling in a healthy way? Creative activities like drawing, painting, or writing stories or poems can be great outlets. They allow you to pour your feelings into something beautiful or imaginative.

Talking things out with someone can also be incredibly helpful. Notice I said to talk things out with someone and not take things out on someone. This could be friends, family, or a trusted adult. Speaking your feelings aloud can clarify what you're actually feeling and why, and it offers the opportunity to receive comfort and advice. Remember, reaching out isn't a sign of weakness; it's a smart way to handle what you're going through. Feeling annoyed with your mom, dad, or sibling? Remember that these emotions are completely normal, and what's important is acknowledging that you are feeling annoyed (probably for a very silly reason) and voicing your feelings to that person. "I know you aren't doing anything on purpose, but right now, what you are doing is really making me feel annoyed, so I'm going to walk away so I don't say something I don't mean." This gives you space to get over it and doesn't make a loved one feel bad.

I've watched tween girls be mean to their parents, yell at their parents, or roll their eyes—and this is not ok. On one hand, I get it. You sometimes treat the people you love the most in the world the worst because you know they aren't going anywhere. But wouldn't it feel better to treat the people you love most in the world the best all the time because you know they aren't going anywhere? Voicing how you are feeling or what is making you feel that way takes the power out of the emotion and will save an outburst later on.

Seeking Support

Finally, know when and how to seek support. If your emotions start to feel overwhelming, or if you find they're impacting your daily life—like your sleep, schoolwork, or relationships—it might be time to reach out for more support. Navigating your emotions during puberty can be challenging, but remember, you're not alone. Every girl goes through this, and with the right tools and support, you can emerge feeling stronger and more self-aware. So, take a deep breath, give yourself grace, and prepare to meet each emotional wave with confidence. You've got this, and we're all here cheering you on!

Anger and Frustration: Healthy Ways to Cope

Everyone experiences anger and frustration at some point, and it's perfectly okay to feel these emotions. They're a natural part of being human, especially when your body and mind are going through a lot of changes, like during puberty. But knowing how to handle these feelings effectively can help you maintain harmony in your relationships and peace within yourself.

Recognizing Triggers

First, let's explore what might trigger your anger or frustration. These emotions often don't come out of nowhere—they're usually sparked by specific situations or actions. For instance, maybe you feel frustrated when you think you're not being heard or angry when you feel unfairly treated. It can also be little things—maybe your sibling borrows your things without asking, you're dealing with a lot of homework, or someone ate that piece of lemon cake leftover from dinner last night that you have been thinking about all day!

Identifying these triggers is like being a detective in your own life. It involves observing yourself and noting what scenarios or actions make you angry or frustrated. This awareness is powerful. Once you know what sets off these emotions, you can start to work on strategies to manage them before they boil over. Sometimes, knowing what triggers your anger is enough to take the sting out of the situation, as you can mentally prepare yourself to face it when it happens.

Coping Mechanisms

So, how can you cope when you feel these strong emotions bubbling up inside you? Let's talk about some strategies that can help. First, think about what made you feel that way. Did someone do something intentionally, or are you perhaps taking something the wrong way? Someone intentionally doing something to hurt you is very different from someone doing something that you took the wrong way. The intentional way is a different conversation with the person than the unintentional way, which is a conversation informing someone about what they did and how it made you feel, right? (You will find that most people aren't doing things to hurt others intentionally; they are just acting without realizing how they are impacting others).

Deep breathing is a wonderful tool. It sounds simple, but it's incredibly effective. When you feel anger rising, take a moment to breathe deeply. Inhale slowly through your nose, hold that breath for a few seconds, then exhale slowly through your mouth. Repeat this a few times. This helps slow down your heart rate and sends a signal to your brain to calm down. It's like hitting the pause button, giving you a chance to collect your thoughts before reacting.

Physical activity is another excellent way to manage anger and frustration. When you're physically active, your body releases endorphins, which are chemicals in the brain that act as natural painkillers and mood elevators. Going for a brisk walk, dancing to your favorite music, or even doing some quick stretches can help release the tension that builds up when you're angry or frustrated.

Talking things out is also crucial. Sometimes, just voicing what you feel can lighten the burden. Talk to someone you trust—a friend, a family member, or a teacher. They might not be able to solve the problem for you, but just having someone listen can make a big difference. They might also offer perspectives or solutions that you hadn't considered.

Channeling Emotions

Finally, finding positive ways to channel your anger and frustration can transform these potentially destructive emotions into something constructive. Creative outlets like drawing, writing, or playing music allow you to express your emotions in safe and fulfilling ways. Not only do these activities provide a distraction from the emotions themselves, but they also give you a means to explore and understand your feelings more deeply.

Volunteering is another excellent way to channel your energies positively. Helping others can boost your mood and broaden your perspective, making personal frustrations seem less overwhelming. Whether helping out at a local community center or joining a school project, turning your focus outward can provide a sense of purpose and satisfaction that counterbalances feelings of anger and frustration.

By mastering these strategies, you can navigate through moments of anger and frustration more smoothly and emerge feeling more empowered and in control. Remember, it's not about never feeling angry or frustrated—that's not realistic or healthy. It's about managing these emotions in ways that are constructive for you and respectful to those around you.

Fill up Your Victory Jar

Navigating puberty can sometimes feel like walking a tightrope, uncomfortable and hoping you don't fall down. As your body changes, you might begin to feel differently about yourself. You're not alone in this; many girls experience fluctuations in how they view themselves during these years. The key is to focus on understanding these changes and learning how to maintain or even boost your confidence through them.

One of the first steps to building a positive self-image during this time is practicing self-compassion. It's about being kind to yourself and recognizing that it's okay to not always feel okay about your changing body. Every girl's body responds differently to puberty, and there's no right or wrong way to look. Embracing this can alleviate a lot of the pressure to meet unrealistic standards. And I have to stop here and acknowledge where unrealistic standards even come from—TV, social media, and online videos. These are all fictitious views of other people's lives and have nothing to do with you, your life, or your body.

So, begin by speaking to yourself in a kind and encouraging voice, just as you would to a close friend. When you catch yourself in a spiral of negative thoughts, pause and ask, "Would I say this to my best friend?" or "What would a loved one say to me if they heard me saying this to myself?" You know you would never say those things to a best friend, and you also know a loved one would love you, support you, and say uplifting things. Hopefully, this pause in your negative thoughts and this simple practice can shift your internal dialogue to be more supportive and loving.

Focusing on your strengths is another powerful strategy. Each person brings their unique skills and qualities to the table. Maybe you're an excellent writer, a thoughtful listener, or someone with a knack for solving puzzles. These abilities are a significant part of who you are and don't change, no matter what your body looks like. Spend some time reflecting on what you do well and the positive traits you possess to fill up your victory jar. Maybe even make a list and add to it regularly. This can be a comforting reminder of your worth, especially when you're feeling down.

Now, consider how often you find yourself comparing your looks, abilities, and achievements with others, especially in this age of social media, where everyone's life seems picture-perfect. It's a trap that can quickly pull down your self-esteem. A helpful way to shift out of this mindset is to focus on appreciating your unique qualities and journey. Put down the screen, celebrate what makes you different, and embrace your individuality. This might mean unfollowing social media accounts that make you feel inadequate or spending less time online. Instead, invest that time in activities that make you feel good about yourself—perhaps drawing, playing a sport, or learning a new skill.

Celebrating small achievements and milestones is crucial in building and maintaining self-esteem. Did you finally nail that math problem that had been bugging you? Or maybe you stood up in front of the class for a presentation, even though it made you nervous. Those are victory jar materials and victories worth recognizing! Take a moment to celebrate these wins, no matter how small they seem. Each one is a stepping stone in your path of growth and a testament to your abilities and courage. Your victory jar represents a place where you drop notes of your daily wins or perhaps share these moments with friends or family who can cheer you on. Celebrating these achievements helps build a positive feedback loop in your mind, reinforcing that you are capable and competent.

Body Image: Loving Yourself through Changes

Understanding what body image means is like unraveling a complex map of how we see ourselves and how we think others see us. Essentially, body image is your perception of your physical appearance. It's the mental picture you have of your body, along with feelings and thoughts that result from that perception. During puberty, this image can go through as many changes as your body does. As your body starts to develop, whether it's getting taller, gaining curves, or facing acne, how you perceive these changes can significantly affect how you feel about yourself. For some, these changes are a welcome part of growing up, but for others, they might be a source of anxiety and discomfort.

One of the biggest influences on how you perceive these changes often comes from outside sources, particularly the media. Every day, whether through movies, television shows, social media, or magazines, you're bombarded with images and messages about what is considered "beautiful" or "desirable." These portrayals can often be unrealistic or highly edited, presenting an ideal that is typically impossible to meet. It's easy to feel like you need to measure up to these standards to be accepted or valued, which can skew your perception of your body.

That's why it's so important to engage with these media sources carefully. This means consuming what's presented to you and thinking actively about it. Ask yourself:

- Are these images realistic?
- Do they represent different types of beauty, including the kind that looks like me?
- Who benefits from me believing I should look a certain way?

- Understanding that these images are often designed to sell products or ideas can help you distance yourself from them and reduce their impact on your self-image.

Seeking out positive influences can also play a crucial role in fostering a healthy body image. This includes surrounding yourself with friends and family who support and uplift you rather than judge or criticize. It also means finding role models who promote a healthy and inclusive definition of beauty. These could be public figures, content creators, or even characters in books and movies who embrace diverse body types and encourage self-acceptance. By filling your environment with positive affirmations and diverse representations of beauty, you reinforce the idea that beauty comes in all shapes, sizes, and colors and that your value is not tied to how closely you fit a certain mold.

Moreover, engaging in activities that make you feel good about your body for its functionality rather than its appearance can be incredibly empowering. This might include sports, dance, yoga, or anything that helps you appreciate what your body can do. Celebrating these capabilities helps shift the focus from how your body looks to what it can achieve, fostering a sense of appreciation and respect for all the amazing things your body is capable of.

Remember, the changes you're experiencing are a normal part of growing up. They don't define your worth or your ability to achieve great things. By understanding what body image is, critically engaging with media, seeking out positive influences, and appreciating your body for what it can do, you're taking important steps toward loving yourself through all the changes. Embrace this time of transformation with kindness and patience toward yourself, and carry forward the confidence that comes from knowing your body is perfect, just as it is, in every stage of its journey.

Pop Quiz

Hey there! Ready to put your emotional intelligence to the test with a fun quiz? Let's see how you might handle different scenarios that could stir up feelings of anger or low self-esteem. Remember, there are no wrong answers here—just opportunities to explore positive ways to manage those tricky emotions. Let's dive in!

Question 1: You've just received a lower grade than expected on a project you worked really hard on. You feel your cheeks getting hot, and frustration starts to build up. What's the best way to handle this situation?

A) Keep quiet and let your anger simmer all day.
B) Complain loudly in class about how unfair it is.
C) Ask your teacher privately for feedback and ways you could improve next time.
D) Decide you're just bad at the subject and give up trying.

Correct Answer: C) Asking for feedback shows a proactive approach. It helps you learn from the experience and can turn feelings of frustration into opportunities for growth.

Question 2: Imagine you're at a sleepover, and some friends start joking about another friend's fashion choice, which is very similar to your style. You start feeling self-conscious and a bit hurt. How should you respond?

A) Laugh along and pretend it doesn't bother you.
B) Change your style to fit in with the others.
C) Defend your friend's and your own style choices, explaining why you like them.
D) Stay quiet and feel bad about your fashion sense.

Correct Answer: C) Standing up for your friend and your own choices boosts your self-esteem and sets a positive example of confidence and respect for others' opinions.

Question 3: You're in a group project, and two members are arguing, neither willing to compromise, and this makes you feel stuck and stressed. What's a constructive way to diffuse the tension?

   A) Wait it out and hope they'll stop eventually.
   B) Take sides and help argue one point of view.
   C) Suggest a break, then discuss how everyone's ideas might be combined.
   D)Tell them you won't work with them unless they stop arguing.

Correct Answer: C) Suggesting a break and then finding a compromise can help calm the situation and shows leadership in resolving conflicts without escalating emotions.

Question 4: You overhear someone making fun of your performance in gym class today. You start to feel embarrassed and angry. What's the healthiest way to manage these feelings?

   A) Confront the person angrily and demand an apology.
   B) Avoid gym class to escape further embarrassment.
   C) Talk to a friend or a trusted adult about how it made you feel.
   D) Make fun of someone else to divert attention.

Correct Answer: C) Discussing your feelings with someone supportive can help you process the situation better and regain your confidence without the situation escalating.

Question 5: You tried out for the school play but didn't get the role you wanted. You feel disappointed and start doubting your acting skills. How should you handle these feelings of self-doubt?

　　A) Decide acting isn't for you and quit.
　　B) Talk to the director about why you weren't chosen and ask for tips on improving.
　　C) Ignore your feelings and pretend everything is fine.
　　D) Blame the director for not recognizing your talent.

Correct Answer: B) Seeking constructive feedback can help you understand the decision and focus on improving, which is much more productive than giving up or harboring resentment.

Question 6: Your science fair project doesn't look as polished as some of your classmates'. You start to feel like it's not good enough and worry about what others will think. What's the best way to boost your confidence?

　　A) Hide your project in the back of the room.
　　B) Criticize others' projects to make yours look better.
　　C) Focus on the effort you put in and be ready to explain your interesting findings.
　　D) Skip the fair to avoid any negative comments.

Correct Answer: C) Emphasizing the hard work you put into your project and the knowledge you gained can help shift your focus from comparison to personal achievement and learning.

Navigating emotions isn't always easy, but understanding how to react positively can make a huge difference in how you feel about yourself and interact with others. Each scenario offers a chance to practice resilience and empathy—key ingredients for emotional growth. Remember, it's all about learning, growing, and finding the best ways to express and manage your feelings.

SEVEN

Friendships and Relationships

Imagine you're painting a picture of your life, and each brushstroke represents a person who has touched your life in some way. Just like colors can blend and change on a canvas, the people in our lives can also change. Friendships, especially during the years of puberty, are like the colors in our painting—they may shift shades, blend with others, or sometimes fade away, making room for new hues to be added. This chapter delves into the art of friendships during such transformative years, guiding you through the ebb and flow of relationships.

Changing Friendships: Growing Apart and Together

Normalizing Change

As you find yourself in the midst of puberty, your body is changing, and your social world may be shifting dramatically, too. It's like being in a garden where the landscape constantly evolves—new flowers bloom, some old ones fade, and the garden's layout might change with the seasons. Similarly, your interests, activities, and even your views on life can transform as you grow. These changes naturally affect your friendships.

It's completely normal for friendships to evolve as you and your friends grow and discover new parts of yourselves. Some friends will grow with you, sharing in your new adventures and changes, while with others, you might find less in common than you once did. Remember, this is a natural part of life—not just now, but always. It's okay to feel sad about drifting apart from someone, but it's also exciting to think about the new friends who will enter your life, bringing with them new experiences and joy.

Maintaining Friendships

Keeping friendships strong through these changing times requires some nurturing, much like keeping a plant healthy. Open communication is key, and when I say communication, I mean talking out loud to each other. Texting, DMing, liking, or emailing is not open communication—it never was and never will be. Be honest with your friends about your feelings, interests, and concerns. It's like watering a plant—you need to pay attention and care regularly.

Plan activities that you can do together in person. Whether it's a weekly sports game, a movie night, or a craft afternoon, shared experiences can strengthen bonds. These activities don't always have to be elaborate. Sometimes, just walking home from school together regularly can give you a chance to connect and share parts of your day.

Letting Go

Sometimes, no matter how much you water a plant, it may not thrive. Similarly, some friendships might naturally come to an end. This can be one of the toughest parts to handle. If a friendship no longer feels supportive, positive, or healthy, it might be time to let go. This doesn't mean you have to end everything abruptly or with hard feelings. Gradually spending less time together and investing more in other friendships can be a gentle way of moving on. Remember, it's important to surround yourself with people who make you feel good about yourself and support you.

Making New Friends

Just as some friendships fade, there's always room for new ones to blossom. Making new friends can be exciting but also a bit intimidating. Start by looking for people who share your interests. Think about the clubs, teams, or groups you are already involved in—these are great places to meet people who like the same things you do. When you share common interests, starting conversations and building connections can be easier and more natural.

Be open to friendships with people who might be different from your current friends. They can introduce you to new perspectives and experiences, adding rich, new colors to the canvas of your life. Be yourself, be kind, and be curious about others. Friendships often start from a simple "hello" or a shared smile. Remember, every friend was once a stranger!

Navigating the changing landscape of relationships during puberty can be as challenging as it is rewarding. By understanding and accepting that changes are part of growing up, maintaining open communication with your friends, knowing when it might be time to move on, and being open to new friendships, you are setting yourself up for a vibrant and supportive social life. Like a garden, your social landscape will continue to grow and change, and that's not just okay—it's beautiful.

Finding Your Support Circle: Peers, Family, and Beyond

Building a strong support network is like creating your own personal team where each member plays a special role in helping you grow and flourish, especially during times as transformative as puberty. Think about it like this: Everyone needs a cheering squad, a group of people who you can turn to when you need advice, when you're feeling down, or when you have great news to share. This network can include friends going through similar experiences, family members who love and support you, and mentors who provide guidance and encouragement.

Firstly, consider the peers in your life. Friends who are also navigating the ups and downs of growing up can be invaluable. This shared experience can create a strong bond and provide a sense of belonging and understanding that's hard to find elsewhere. Whether it's talking about your first crush or figuring out how to manage your time with all the new schoolwork, having friends to discuss these topics with can make the transitions of puberty much less intimidating. Plus, as you support each other, you'll find that your problems might seem a bit smaller when you see them through the lens of helping someone else.

However, it's not just about having people to talk to; it's also about building trust within these relationships. Trust is the foundation of any strong support network. It's knowing that you can share your feelings and experiences without judgment and that what you share will be kept confidential unless you decide otherwise. This trust must be mutual. Just as you need to feel safe to share your thoughts and feelings, you need to provide a safe space for your friends, too. It's like having a secret garden where everything you discuss is protected by the walls of respect and confidentiality you've built together.

By weaving together these various threads of support—peers who understand, family members who care, and mentors who guide—you create a robust tapestry of relationships. This network not only supports you through the challenges of puberty but also enriches your journey, making it a shared experience filled with learning, growth, and mutual support. Remember, no one has to manage everything on their own. Having a circle of support is like having a team where every member brings something unique to the table, helping you navigate life with more confidence and joy.

The Role of Siblings during Puberty: Allies or Annoyances?

I am the oldest of four daughters in my family. I can honestly say that the answer to that question is "both." When I was in my teen years, my sibling, who was closest in age, was definitely an annoyance because I really didn't know how to talk about what was going on in my life (I know she felt the same way), but today she is my best friend, and we are so alike. My younger siblings were not so much of an annoyance because they were just little kids who wanted to play, so I didn't have to think about anything but playing and smiling with them. But, again, today, they are my best friends.

As you navigate through the waves of changes during puberty, your relationship with your siblings might also experience its own shifts and turns. It's like suddenly finding yourself in a dance where both of you are trying to lead—sometimes stepping on each other's toes, sometimes moving in perfect harmony. During puberty, you're not just dealing with your own growth and emotions; you're also interacting with siblings who may be going through their own significant changes. This can lead to a mix of conflicts and deepened bonds as each of you evolves.

Let's talk about the dynamics between you and your siblings during these years. It's common for conflicts to arise more frequently. Perhaps you're feeling that your younger sibling is too clingy at a time when you crave more privacy. Or maybe an older sibling seems more critical, just when you're feeling most sensitive. These conflicts often stem from the fact that you and your siblings are exploring new identities and testing personal and relational boundaries. You might feel like your sibling doesn't understand you anymore, or you may get annoyed more quickly by things that didn't bother you before.

However, it's important to recognize that these changes are part of growing up, and they don't mean your relationships are falling apart. Instead, they're stretching and reshaping. Acknowledging that both of you are going through significant changes can help reduce the frustration. It helps to have a conversation about these feelings when you're both calm, explaining how you're feeling and listening to their side of the story, too. This mutual understanding can ease tensions and make navigating this dance a bit smoother.

Respecting Differences

As you both grow, respecting each other's differences becomes crucial. You might be into books and quiet evenings, while your sibling is all about sports and being outdoors. Instead of letting these differences create a wedge between you, use them as opportunities to learn from each other. Show interest in what your sibling loves—you might find yourself enjoying a new book genre they recommend, or they might discover they like your favorite sport.

Setting boundaries is also part of respecting differences. If you need more privacy, gently explain this to them. Use clear, respectful language to communicate your needs: "I really need some quiet time in the evenings to unwind. Can we hang out together after dinner instead?" By respecting each other's space and needs, you foster a healthier, more respectful relationship.

Communicating with Parents and Adults: Tips for Open Conversations

Opening up to parents or other trusted adults about the changes and challenges you're experiencing can sometimes feel like stepping onto a stage without knowing your lines. It's completely natural to feel a bit nervous or unsure about how to start these conversations, especially about topics as personal as puberty, emotions, and relationships. But I don't want you to overthink this too much. Did you know your parents love you more than anything in the world and want nothing more than to help you, hug you, and tell you everything will be alright? Believe me, they will be so open to questions and dialogue on any subject with you, so don't worry too much about this. Having open, honest talks with adults can bring comfort, insights, and support that make navigating this phase of life a bit easier. Here are some strategies to help you initiate and make the most of these important discussions.

Starting the Conversation

Finding the right moment to talk can sometimes be half the battle. Look for a time when both you and the adult you want to talk to aren't rushed or distracted. This might be during a car ride, taking a walk, while making dinner together, or after finishing a movie. These less formal settings can make the conversation feel more natural and relaxed. You can start with something simple and straightforward, like, "Can we talk? There are some things on my mind about growing up that I feel unsure about."

If you're feeling anxious about bringing up more sensitive topics, you might find it helpful to ease into these discussions with something less intense. For example, talking about a friend's experience or a scenario from a TV show can be a way to introduce the subject without feeling too exposed right away.

Expressing Needs and Concerns

Remember, it's okay to express that you're finding certain aspects of growing up confusing or difficult. It's ok that you may not know how to say it right, but if you stay in the conversation, you will get there. Adults in your life can often provide reassurance, share their own experiences, and offer advice from a place of love and understanding. They were once in your shoes, and reminding them of that can sometimes help bridge gaps in understanding.

Seeking Advice and Support

Adults with more life experience can provide perspectives and insights that might not be obvious to someone going through these experiences for the first time. Whether it's coping with mood swings, dealing with a challenging friendship, or understanding physical changes, asking clear questions can help the adult provide targeted advice that is more likely to be helpful.

It's also important to recognize that adults are not all-knowing and might not always have all the answers. Sometimes, they might suggest seeking additional resources or support together, such as talking to a healthcare provider or counselor or looking up information from reliable sources. This can be a shared journey of discovery, enhancing your relationship, and providing mutual learning opportunities.

Understanding Different Perspectives

Always be kind. Navigating these conversations with patience and an open heart can sometimes lead to surprising discoveries about each other. Through these dialogues, mutual understanding is forged, building a foundation of trust and support that can help guide you through the ups and downs of growing up.

Remember, the goal of these conversations is to seek information and advice and deepen your connection with the adults in your life, creating a support system based on mutual respect and understanding.

Pop Quiz

Hey, are you ready for a quick quiz that's all about making the best out of your family relationships? These questions are designed to help you think about how you can involve your sibling or parents more in your conversations, especially during these rollercoaster years of puberty. Remember, it's all about building stronger bonds and opening up new channels for communication. Let's get started!

Question 1: You've learned something new and interesting about handling stress during puberty in health class. How could you use this information at home?

> A) Keep the information to yourself; it's just for school.
> B) Share the tips with your parents and discuss ways to implement them at home.
> C) Make a poster for your room as a personal reminder.
> D) Use the information to start a health blog for teens.

Correct Answer: B) Sharing what you've learned with your parents is a great way to educate them about what you're experiencing and open up a dialogue about how you can all support each other. Discussing these new strategies together can bring new understanding and cooperation to your family dynamics, making home a supportive environment for managing stress.

Question 2: Your younger sibling seems upset about starting middle school next year and is worried about making new friends. How can you use your own experiences to help them?

A) Tell them to just wait and see how it goes.
B) Share your own story of starting middle school and what you learned about making friends.
C) Suggest they talk to their teacher about it.
D) Buy them a book about making friends.

Correct Answer: B) Sharing your own experiences can be incredibly reassuring. Talk about your first day, how you felt, and what strategies helped you make new friends. This shows them that their feelings are normal and gives them practical advice from someone they trust. It's a great way to boost their confidence and show that you're there for them.

Navigating the complexities of family relationships during puberty can be challenging but also deeply rewarding. These quiz questions are designed to encourage you to think about how you can involve your family more in your life, especially when things seem tough. By opening up to your family, you gain their support and strengthen your relationships, making your family a cornerstone of your support system during these formative years.

As we wrap up this chapter on navigating friendships and family relationships, remember that these connections are crucial during your growth. They provide love, support, and a sense of belonging.

EIGHT

Creating Your Personal Puberty Diary— a Space for Thoughts and Questions

We have covered a lot in this book so far. Beginning at the beginning, we covered puberty, then periods, bras, hair and skin care, changing friendships, exercise, and nutrition! You probably have a lot of thoughts on all these new topics to review. So, let's get those thoughts out of your head and into a safe place that you can review later or use as a platform to have harder conversations with a trusted adult. I've mentioned a lot about journaling prior, so let's dive into what a journal could look like.

Benefits of Journaling

Imagine having a special space where you can whisper all your secrets, unpack your day, and navigate the maze of emotions and changes that come with growing up. That's what keeping a personal diary can be like. It's your private area to express yourself freely, explore your feelings, and make sense of the world around you and the changes within you. One of the beautiful things about journaling is that it's a form of self-expression that accepts your words just as they are, whether they're messy, ecstatic, confused, or curious.

Writing down what happens during your day, how you feel about the changes to your body, or even documenting your dreams and fears can provide relief and, sometimes, a new perspective. It's like the diary holds up a mirror to your inner world, helping you understand yourself better. This can be particularly comforting during times when everything else seems in flux. Plus, the act of writing can soothe your nerves and reduce stress—think of it as a quiet time just for you, where you can unwind and get all those tangled thoughts out of your head and onto paper.

What to Include

Your puberty diary can be as unique as you are, and you can decide what goes into it. Start with daily reflections, which can be simple descriptions of your day, how you felt about certain events, or your interactions with friends and family. You can also jot down any questions you have about the changes happening to your body or emotions you're experiencing. It's also helpful to track patterns, like your mood swings or physical changes, as this can help you identify what triggers certain emotions or reactions (which we talked about in an earlier chapter).

Besides these, consider including what you are excited about. What are you nervous about? You can also make a habit of noting the things you're grateful for each day. Gratitude journaling can shift your focus from worries and uncertainties to positive aspects of your life, enhancing your overall well-being. Being grateful doesn't have to be big things either. They can be the simplest of things that make you happy. For example, you can be happy that you smelled freshly mown grass that day or saw a fluffy cloud that looked like a dog taking a poop and made you laugh.

Reflecting on Growth

Every now and then, take some time to look back on your previous entries. This can be incredibly rewarding and eye-opening. You'll see how much you've grown, how your feelings and thoughts have evolved, and how you've navigated the challenges that once seemed daunting. This reflection can foster a deep sense of accomplishment and boost your self-awareness. It's like looking back at a map of a journey you've traveled, realizing just how far you've come, and seeing more clearly the path ahead.

As you continue to fill the pages of your diary, remember that this book is a witness to your transformation—a transformation unique to you. It's a place where you can always speak your truth, explore your feelings, and dream your biggest dreams while knowing that it's a journey you're well-equipped to handle, one word at a time.

Homework

Creating your puberty diary is like planting a garden of words that grows alongside you. As you step into this personal space where you can express yourself freely, let's sprinkle some ideas to help you start. Your diary entries can be as diverse as the thoughts and feelings you experience each day, and here are five fresh prompts to help you begin this reflective adventure.

Firstly, think about your changing friendships. Puberty can sometimes shuffle the characters in your life's story, bringing some friends closer and perhaps moving others further away. Write about a friendship that has changed recently—how has it changed? Do you miss how it used to be, or are you excited about how it's transforming?

Next, your body is going through many changes, and documenting these shifts can be really interesting. Choose one physical change you've noticed, whether it's something visible like your height or something less apparent like your changing voice. How do you feel about this change? What's exciting about it, and what might be a bit challenging?

Then, consider your emotional responses to everyday situations, which might be more intense or different than before. Maybe you've reacted strongly to things that didn't bother you much before. Write about a recent event that triggered a strong emotional response. What happened? How did you feel? Reflecting on these moments can help you better understand and manage your feelings as you grow.

Lastly, dive into a daydream. Allow yourself to drift into your imagination and describe a perfect day. Who are you with? What are you doing? How do you feel throughout this day? Daydreaming can be a delightful escape and a window into what makes you truly happy and relaxed. Plus, it's just fun to imagine wonderful scenarios and perhaps find ways to make some of them a reality.

By starting with these diverse journal prompts, your diary will soon become a rich tapestry of your experiences, thoughts, and dreams during puberty. It's a space where you can be entirely yourself, express your innermost thoughts, and navigate the complexities of growing up with a trusted companion—your diary.

So keep your diary close, your communication open, and your support network strong. The adventure is just beginning, and there's so much more to discover and understand about yourself and the world around you.

NINE

Navigating Social Media and Digital Communication

This chapter is extremely important to me because I want you to acknowledge where you are in your life so far. Where is that, you ask? You are still learning how to be a human in the real world, and truthfully, it will take you well into your 20s to feel confident in the real world. Even then, you are still constantly learning. That's where you are right now—learning the real world.

Then you've got the digital world, which is not the same. It's an entirely new world with different expectations, language, and communications. In my perfect world, kids would only be able to engage in this world once you are well into your late teens (graduated high school). I'm not saying don't have a phone to make phone calls—I'm just saying only have a smartphone once you graduate high school. A phone for calling (friends or family) and texting only (to direct family members, not friends) is appropriate at your age—again, my opinion. I know my opinion is not common, but there you have it.

I don't think you need to worry about a digital world until you are more equipped with life skills. But you are probably thinking, *What about my friends?* It feels like everyone has a phone with access to social media, right? It might feel that way, and I challenge you to find friends without their noses in a phone. If you are one of those kids that doesn't have a phone, be proud of that! Shout from the rooftops about that, and you will find others.

Let's think about the real world versus the digital world. Here is how I would compare the real world to the digital world. Imagine your parents putting you into a taxi cab, paying the driver, and saying, "Drop her off in New York City." Then, your parents turn to you and say, "Have fun, find your way home, and we'll see you then." What? Your parents would never do that in the real world, right? You betcha they wouldn't! But allowing you to have access to the internet and social media, unsupervised and without conversation on everything you are seeing, is basically the same thing. I want to emphasize that I don't think parents do this on purpose because, in our experience (I am your parent's age) in this digital world, that's not even 20 years old, we are still learning too. We are learning more every day. But I want to call this comparison out to parents because it's accurate.

Many people don't know that these social media feeds are programmed to figure out your likes and continuously bring videos and images of those things to your viewing screen. They are programmed to keep you on your phone and engage in its content. It is purposefully messing with you to keep you engaged in that social media feed. Do you like videos of puppies and kittens (who doesn't)? Once you watch one of those videos, you will now get a constant feed of them coming your way. Good luck turning off a puppy video! This is why I say if you aren't exposed to this yet, thank your lucky stars and keep that going for as long as you can. You can find a puppy video on America's Funniest Home Videos Animal Edition with Alfonso instead. If you are exposed to this digital world already, start paying attention to what keeps making its way in front of you.

I know this feels like a pretty negative portrayal of social media and the digital world, but at your age, it does not help you or your development to engage in these things. Call your friends to talk, and don't fall into the trap of texting mindless chatter or emojis for hours because you can. I don't think that social media is the devil, though, but the approach to it needs to be deliberate and intentional. With that said, I want to share what I can about helping you navigate the digital world if you find yourself there at this age. Most importantly, ask your parents questions and talk about what you see.

Parents: Review your child's texts, emails, and social media feeds daily, and talk with your children about what they saw, what it means, and how it made them feel.

Social Media: Understanding Its Impact on Self-Image

Unfortunately, navigating the digital landscape of social media is a significant part of daily life for many young girls like you. In fact, research, including studies from sources like the Pew Research Center, shows that a vast majority of tweens engage on platforms like Instagram, TikTok, and Snapchat every single day (Vogels, Emily A. "Teens and Social Media: Key Findings from Pew Research Center Surveys" Pew Research, April 23, 2023. https://www.pewresearch.org/short-reads/2023/04/24/teens-and-social-media-key-findings-from-pew-research-center-surveys/). These platforms aren't just spaces for sharing selfies and updates; they have become a central hub for communication, entertainment, and information.

As you scroll through these feeds, you're constantly bombarded with images and videos that might seem perfect. Picture-perfect lifestyles, flawless "beauty," and endless happiness dominate these platforms, all meticulously curated and often enhanced by filters and editing tools. It's easy to forget that what you see isn't always the full story. These snapshots are just highlights, not the behind-the-scenes of someone's life. They often don't reflect the ordinary moments that everyone experiences. Continuously looking at these feeds can trick you and your perception of normal and heavily influence how you feel about your life and appearance. Think of the digital world as a highlight reel, made up of only the great moments in someone's life only. Compare this to a real-life family photo album—as you flip through the pages, the only pictures you will find in there are birthdays, vacations, first days of school, picnics, weddings, baby showers, anniversaries, or graduations. And when was the last time you went to a friend's house and said, "Hey, let's get your family photo album out?" Probably never, but seeing it on social media makes that suddenly cool. You don't see the picture of you watching Sesame Street on the couch in the morning with a bowl of cereal, sitting around the dinner table at night with your family, or a hug or snuggle when you just hurt yourself. Now that's normal and 99% of everyone's life—the average, normal, and mundane makes each of our lives and experiences unique and beautiful. Getting wrapped up in social media so young will make you forget to look around and appreciate your life and what is right in front of you.

Critical Media Literacy

This is where critical media literacy comes into play. It's an essential skill that helps you critically understand and analyze media content, recognizing biases, underlying messages, and the real intentions behind posts. By questioning the content you are viewing and consuming—asking yourself:

- Who created it?
- Why was it created?
- What message it's trying to convey?

You can start to differentiate between realistic portrayals and styled, filtered, and edited presentations. This critical approach helps protect your self-esteem and promotes a healthier, more realistic understanding of life and success.

If you are going to engage on social media, choose what kind of content you interact with. Be deliberate about your choices. Choose uplifting, motivational, and positive messages about life. At your age, stay away from feeds that only talk about fashion or "beauty." Why? You are still figuring out your own fashion and your own version of "beauty" (which is different for everyone). Don't let someone else decide those things for you in a digital world. You figure it out in the real world first.

Moreover, it's so easy to fall into the trap of comparing yourself to what you see in the virtual world. It's crucial to remind yourself that your value isn't determined by "likes" or online popularity. Focusing on self-love and personal growth involves appreciating yourself as you are and recognizing your achievements and qualities without comparing them to others, and this happens in real life. Celebrate your real-life moments—those genuine, unfiltered experiences that bring you joy and satisfaction. Again, I point out here that at your age, you are still figuring out your strengths and value in the real world. The digital world will be there when you are ready (graduated high school), and entering into the digital world as a strong, confident person with intention will be a much more positive experience.

Lastly, promoting body positivity shouldn't just stay online. Carrying these values into your home and school life is important. Encourage open discussions about body image and media perceptions with your friends and family. Campaigns like those by the Dove Self-Esteem Project provide excellent resources and support for fostering self-esteem and challenging beauty stereotypes. By being part of these conversations, you contribute to a broader change, helping create an environment where everyone can feel accepted and valued, regardless of how they look or what they achieve on social media.

Navigating social media wisely and healthily is like learning to navigate New York City, where your parents just sent you off in a cab. Are you ready for that at your age? The answer should be no, so consider staying away from or reducing your social media time for a few years. If you answered yes, then you know that by understanding New York City's layout, choosing your routes deliberately and with intention, and appreciating each genuine corner, you can enjoy the journey without losing sight of who you are and the incredible value you bring to the world, both online and off.

Deep Dive: Social Media and Body Image

Studies, like those published in the journal *Body Image (https://www.sciencedirect.com)*, have found a direct link between exposure to celebrity and influencer imagery and feelings of inadequacy or poor body image among tweens. Every time you see a photo of a model with a seemingly perfect body or a flawless lifestyle, your own wonderful qualities might feel less significant.

But how widespread is this issue? According to reports from Common Sense Media, many tweens admit that social media has shaped their self-image (https://www.commonsensemedia.org/articles/how-can-media-affect-kids-body-image). Many say that how they look is crucially important, and much of this pressure comes from the relentless stream of perfect, filtered, and edited images they encounter online. This constant barrage of perfection can make everyday "beauty" and real-world accomplishments seem ordinary and undervalued. Social media is not real life, yet tween girls start to believe that it is, and their value becomes tied to it. Social media is not real life.

This is where critical media literacy comes into play again. Understanding the dynamics is the first step in reclaiming your self-image from the clutches of unrealistic standards. It's about more than just knowing these effects—it's about actively understanding how you interact with digital content. Choose to engage with social media in a way that uplifts and supports your well-being. These choices can help create a digital environment that celebrates realness over perfection, diversity over uniformity, and personal growth over superficial popularity.

Remember, the images and lives portrayed online are often just snippets of reality, carefully chosen and polished. Your value doesn't diminish because of what you see online; instead, it deepens with every real experience, every genuine laugh, and every true connection you make.

Impact of Text Messaging and Emails

In today's digital age, text messaging and emails have become commonplace tools for communication, especially among schools and tweens. They're quick, easy, and let you stay connected with friends and family anytime and anywhere. However, these forms of communication come with their challenges, particularly when it comes to misunderstandings and the emotional impact they can have. Unlike face-to-face conversations, where you can see someone's expressions and hear their tone of voice, text messages and emails lack this emotional context. This absence can most often lead to misunderstandings or anxiety, especially about sensitive topics like body image, friendships, and self-presentation.

Imagine you receive a message from a friend that reads, *That outfit was interesting you wore to school today.* Without hearing their tone or seeing their facial expression, it's tough to know if they mean it in a positive, sarcastic, or critical way. This unknown can lead to anxiety as you try to interpret their words, often assuming the worst. Overall, digital communications can increase the risk of misinterpretation, uncertainty, and emotional distress. It is no secret that messages can be easily misconstrued without the nonverbal cues of traditional face-to-face interactions, leading to feelings of insecurity or doubt, particularly regarding one's self-image or choices. If you want to pay someone a compliment, call them or tell it to their face. If you want to tell someone you don't like their outfit, call them or tell it to their face. That sounds uncomfortable, though, right? It would be so much easier to put that into a text message. Of course, it would, but that's not communication. That's not real life.

Another significant concern with text-based communication is the risk of cyberbullying and body shaming. The anonymity and physical distance digital platforms provide can sometimes embolden individuals to say things they wouldn't say in person. Negative comments about someone's appearance, weight, or clothing choices can be hurtful and damaging, especially when they come through personal channels like text messages or emails where support systems may not immediately see or address these issues. The impact of such experiences can be profound, affecting how you see yourself and interact with others.

To combat these issues, parents and educators must foster open dialogues about the nature of digital communication and its impact on body image and self-esteem. The American Psychological Association recommends creating environments at home and in schools where young people can discuss their online interactions and how they affect their feelings about themselves (American Psychological Association. "Reducing Social Media Use Significantly Improves Body Image in Teens, Young Adults," February 23, 2023. https://www.apa.org/news/press/releases/2023/02/social-media-body-image). These conversations can help you develop healthier relationships with digital media and equip you with strategies to handle negative experiences effectively.

Also, if you have a phone, allowing your parents to view all communications is important. What? Yes, your parents are probably paying for that phone and, therefore, it is technically theirs to do with what they want, but that's not the main reason. At your age, would your parents give you a car and wish you luck in the real world? Absolutely not. Well, a phone has the same type of impact without supervision—it can hurt you and others. So, the cardinal rule as a good human in the real world is if you wouldn't say it in person or you wouldn't want your parents to see or hear you saying it, don't put it into a text message. So it's not only about teaching you how to be a good human during this time when emotions are running high, but it's also about ensuring your emotional welfare is being kept safe in the communications you are receiving. Parents should review this every evening and have conversations with you about them to answer any questions or provide feedback on how a certain message might be misunderstood.

Navigating the complex world of digital communication requires awareness, understanding, and proactive strategies. By recognizing the potential for miscommunication, understanding the risks of cyberbullying, and engaging in open conversations about these topics, you can enjoy the benefits of staying connected while safeguarding your emotional well-being. Remember, the digital world is a tool, and like any tool, learning how to use it effectively makes all the difference.

Setting Boundaries: Healthy Habits for Social Media Use

If you are currently engaged in social media but, after reading what I've said above, feel like maybe it's not the best place for you, or you want to cut back your time there, let's talk about how. It's easy to get swept up (because social media is programmed to keep you online), scrolling endlessly (doom scrolling, I call it), or jumping from one app to another, losing track of time and even your reasons for being online in the first place. Here are some suggested strategies to keep you in a balanced place:

- Setting specific time limits for social media use can be a game-changer. Consider, for instance, setting a timer for 20 minutes of social media (whatever that looks like for you) time after homework and before dinner. You should be sitting near your parent (or trusted adult in charge of your well-being) who might be making the dinner, so if you have questions or your parents hear something, it can be talked about right away. This helps keep your evening structured and ensures that social media doesn't swallow up time you might spend on other activities like reading or spending time with family.
- Take the busy days off of social media altogether. Maybe on Mondays and Wednesdays, you have school, band practice, homework, dinner, and bedtime. Trying to squeeze in social media (for what reason exactly?) may not be the right place to spend your time. Time management will serve you well as you grow older, so starting this skill now can't hurt anything.
- Take days off of social media altogether, whether you are busy or not. You get to spend all day at school with your friends, and when you come home, your family wants to talk to you and spend time with you. It's their turn! So show them some love, help make dinner, or go for a walk. Your friends will be there tomorrow. There is nothing important or life-altering happening on social media. If something was going on that you needed to know, you would get a phone call.
- Leaving your phone at home when you are out with your family. Getting on your phone and doom scrolling social media just because you can might make the loved ones

around you feel like they aren't important to you. Maybe you would rather be with strangers than with them. I'm sure you may have felt that way if you were with an adult who didn't want to play a game but wanted to surf their social media feed instead. It doesn't feel good, right?
- Being intentional about why you're logging on is crucial. Ask yourself: Am I looking for entertainment, trying to connect with friends, or maybe searching for inspiration for a school project? Understanding your motivations can help you use social media more purposefully and prevent you from getting lost in the doom scroll.

The concept of a digital detox, especially one that involves the whole family, can significantly amplify the benefits of these breaks. Even if you aren't engaged in social media, I'm sure you have noticed that all the adults in your life appear to be. Believe me, they would love for you to suggest a digital detox day. Imagine committing to a Saturday without social media—no checking Instagram stories, no tweeting, just you and your loved ones finding fun in the real world. This could mean a family game day, a picnic at the local park, or a creative workshop at home where everyone makes something with their hands. These detox days can help everyone reset their relationships with digital devices, improving mood and well-being. It's a powerful way to remind yourself that while social media is a tool for connection, the world outside the screen has much to offer.

Pop Quiz

Hey there! Ready to test your savvy on how to maintain an accurate view of what social media is and a healthy relationship with it? This quiz is designed to help you reflect on your online choices and how they contribute to a supportive, fun, and safe environment for everyone. Each question is a little puzzle piece that, when put together, will show you how to navigate the social media landscape wisely. No pressure—think of this as a way to explore new ideas and strategies for being a positive presence online!

Question 1: You see a post that makes you feel bad about your appearance. What should you do?

> A) Ignore it and keep scrolling.
> B) Post a negative comment on it.
> C) Reflect on why it affects you and consider unfollowing the account.
> D) Share the post with your friends so they also feel bad.

Correct Answer: C) Reflecting on your feelings helps you understand your triggers, and choosing to unfollow accounts that make you feel insecure can improve your overall social media experience. Show an adult the post and talk it through with them. Apply critical media literacy as well. Who posted it? Why was it posted? What was their intent?

Question 2: All your friends seem to be engaged in social media, and you feel left out. What should you do?

> A) Ask your parents why they choose to keep you off of social media.
> B) Seek out other kids you have things in common with outside the online world.
> C) Think about what makes you happy in the real world and engage more in those things.
> D) Ask one of those kids what they enjoy about social media.

Correct Answer: All of them. Your parents are doing what they think is best for you (and they are right), but understanding their reasons is a great way to open that communication and take a lot of emotion out of it. Believe it or not, many kids only have a phone to call mom and dad for a ride after practice or can only text their parents—no friends. Find those kids and have a conversation about something in the real world. Do you enjoy playing soccer, reading the *Maximum Ride* series by James Patterson, painting, or hiking? Find those kids that enjoy the same and engage with them. Also, I think if you ask most kids why they are on social media, you will find nothing deliberate or intentional about it. It is simply the feeling that "everyone else is on it, so I have to be." Feeling left out is not fun, but if you turn it into your choice to not be on social media—suddenly, you don't feel left out anymore because you are focusing now on what you want to do and where you want to spend your time.

As we wrap up our exploration of social media and digital communication, remember that these tools are just one small part of your larger social experience. While perhaps feeling a bit serious and heavy, this chapter is important to your growth and how you navigate life in general. Puberty kicks up a lot of new things, as you read in Chapters 1 to 7, and focusing on that is enough. Social media is not real life; it is a version of someone else's life and should be kept far away from you until you have your feet solidly planted in the real world in front of you. You are a wonderful young person who is learning every day, so trust the adults in your life to do what's best for you and stay present in the real world.

TEN

Bullying and Peer Pressure

Navigating the social aspects of growing up can sometimes feel like walking a tightrope, balancing your happiness with the desire to fit in. Let's face it: Everyone wants to fit in, but the facts of life are that you will only fit in when you know who you are, what you think, and what you like. Peer pressure and bullying are two challenges that can shake this balance, making you feel as though every step is a potential misstep. Understanding what these experiences look like and knowing how to handle them can help you keep your footing and walk confidently, regardless of the winds of adversity.

Recognizing Bullying and Peer Pressure

Bullying can sneak into your life in various forms, from the more obvious, like being called names or being physically hurt, to the less visible, such as being excluded from groups or cyberbullying, which occurs online. It's crucial to recognize that bullying often involves a repeated pattern of behavior intended to hurt or intimidate someone physically, verbally, or psychologically. Peer pressure, while sometimes less aggressive, can also be damaging. It involves your peers pushing you, explicitly or implicitly, to do something you might not be comfortable with, which can include everything from making fun of or excluding someone else. Both bullying and peer pressure thrive on the intended person's sense of isolation and helplessness, which is why recognizing them early is the first step to addressing them.

Cyberbullying, as we mentioned, occurs online. It is using technology to hurt, embarrass, or threaten others. This can be via text, email, pictures, DMs, social media, or any other technology. And this can be done by a friend or stranger. Unfortunately, sitting behind a phone or computer makes it much easier to throw hurtful comments out there without really having to answer them right away. It is easy for you to receive a message you don't understand or from someone you don't know. I would urge you not to respond and talk to an adult. If you receive a message from a friend you don't understand, call them back and ask them what it means. Going back and forth in a text message to clarify another message is a circle from which there is no exit. Having a fight over text messages is also a waste of time.

This is why it's important to involve your parents in digital reviews at the end of each day so they can see the communication you've received and the communication you've put out into the digital world.

As I've stated before, at your age, your engagement in social media, texting with friends, and emails should be minimal overall. Figuring out yourself in the real world is a challenge enough, particularly at your age when you are emotionally and physically changing and worrying about pads or tampons, sports bra or lace bra, and crying or yelling! It's a lot.

However, if you find yourself engaged in these online environments and feel the need to post something or comment on someone else's post, I urge you to talk to an adult before doing so. Remember the critical media literacy we talked about before:

- Think about why you are posting something (Is it for likes? Are you hoping someone will notice you? Are you celebrating something you are really proud of? Does it need to be posted?)
- What is the intent or message you are trying to put out there? (Are you trying to uplift others after having a hard day? Are you trying to make others laugh? Do you not have a message and just want to post it? Does it need to be posted?)

Adults can help you sort through these questions and develop a healthy view on what should be put online and what shouldn't. Once it's online, it's there forever, so beginning cautiously and with great reservations is the key to a good long-term relationship.

Strategies for Responding

When facing bullying or peer pressure, your response can significantly influence the outcome. One effective approach is asserting yourself confidently, which is easier said than done. If someone pressures you to do something you're uncomfortable with, a firm "no," "no, I'm good," or "no, thank you" can be more powerful than you think. Practice saying these no's in a calm and confident tone. You can also practice other assertive responses in the mirror or with a trusted friend or family member until they feel natural.

Also, seeking help from trusted adults is key. This could be a teacher, a school counselor, or a parent. Sometimes, it's hard to put into words what was done to make you feel a certain way—and that's ok—but talking about the feeling itself is helpful. It's not tattling—it's taking care of your well-being. Adults have more experience and resources to handle these situations and can take actions that protect you and sometimes even the person exerting the pressure or bullying, who might also need help. Did you know that most adults in your life, when they were younger, have experienced some form of bullying and peer pressure? It's true, so don't feel isolated or alone. There is an entire community around you that understands what you are going through and wants to help.

As someone who was bullied when I was younger (before the digital world and through outward name calling) and now watching my daughter go through this herself (through exclusion), I can say with confidence that enlisting the help of your parents and teachers is a powerful tool to help you through this. I know when I was younger, I didn't feel comfortable standing up for myself, nor did I feel comfortable talking to an adult because I let my feelings of isolation get the better of me. My daughter also struggles to stand up for herself because she believes that if she does, she is just as bad as the bullies. Standing up for yourself does not take away your title of being a nice and kind person. It simply allows you to tell others what you will not stand for or what you do not like. Role-playing with my daughter and talking with her teachers has been a game changer for her circumstances, and through constant communication, she feels more empowered every day to take charge of this situation.

So, as I've said many times in this book, talking with a trusted adult is key during this time. Give it a shot—you won't be sorry you did.

Building Resilience

Engage in activities that make you feel good and competent, whether it's sports, arts, or academic achievements. Surround yourself with positive influences and people who appreciate you for who you are. Additionally, learning to manage stress effectively through activities you enjoy or simply talking things out can fortify your emotional defenses. Resilience doesn't mean you won't experience difficulties, but it does equip you to handle them more effectively when they arise.

Supporting Others

Fostering a culture of kindness and respect is essential in combating bullying and peer pressure. If you see someone else being bullied or pressured, stand up for them if it's safe to do so, or report the incident to an adult. Offering your support can make a huge difference to someone who might feel alone and scared. Together, you can create an environment where bullying and peer pressure are called out and dealt with rather than being swept under the rug. Remember, change often starts with the brave actions of a few. By standing up for what's right, you contribute to a safer, more respectful community for everyone.

ELEVEN

Building Confidence and Self-Esteem

Imagine you're the main character in your favorite movie. Every scene, every challenge you face, is part of the plot that makes you—yes, you—the hero of your own story. Like any hero, sometimes you might feel unsure or face tough moments where your confidence dips (did you know this happens to everyone?). But here's the secret: The power to boost your confidence and strengthen your self-esteem is like a superpower, and it's already inside you. This chapter is about activating that power and learning to shine even brighter.

Self-Talk for Self-Esteem: How to Be Your Own Cheerleader

Positive Self-Talk

Let's start with something called positive self-talk. Think of it as being your own cheerleader. It's all about what you say to yourself daily and how these words can shape how you feel and see yourself. For instance, instead of thinking, "I messed up that math test;

I'm no good at math," try shifting to, "That math test was tough, but I'm going to study harder and nail the next one!" See the difference? It's about focusing on solutions and your ability to improve, which boosts your confidence and keeps you motivated.

Positive self-talk isn't just fluffy words; it's backed by science. Psychologists have found it can significantly impact our self-esteem and overall mental health, making us feel more capable and in control (The Pathway 2 Success. "How to Teach Positive Self-Talk," June 15, 2017. https://www.thepathway2success.com/how-to-teach-positive-self-talk/). Every time you catch yourself being a bit too harsh or critical, try to flip the script. Speak to yourself as you would to your best friend—with kindness, encouragement, and belief in your abilities.

Self-Compassion

Being kind to yourself, or showing self-compassion, is like giving yourself a hug when you need it the most. It's about recognizing that it's okay not to be perfect and treating yourself with the same compassion you would offer a friend. If you stumble or face setbacks, instead of being self-critical, be understanding toward yourself. Think about what you would say to a friend in the same situation. You'd likely offer support and understanding, right? Apply that same kindness to yourself.

Self-compassion helps you navigate tough times with a gentler perspective, making challenges less daunting. It allows you to recognize that everyone makes mistakes and that each mistake is a stepping stone to learning and growing.

Daily Affirmations

What is an affirmation? Think of affirmations as your personal cheer squad, always ready to remind you of your strengths and capabilities, especially when you might not feel your best. For instance, on a day when you're feeling grumpy or sad—maybe you are at a certain point in your menstruation—an affirmation like, "My hormones are giving me the business today, and I will be kind to others and do my best," can shift your perspective and give you the energy to keep going. Or, if you ever feel lonely or out of place, reminding yourself, "I am loved and valued just as I am," can provide a great deal of comfort and reassurance.

Now, let's make this practical. I want you to think of three positive affirmations that resonate with you. These should be statements that make you feel empowered and confident. Write them down here in your book. You can pull from these daily or even come back and add new ones as you grow and your goals evolve. This is your personal toolkit for daily encouragement, so make it as vibrant and uplifting as you need!

Daily Affirmation Exercise

By incorporating affirmations into your daily routine, you're not just practicing positive thinking but actively creating a mindset that champions self-belief and resilience. Over time, these affirmations will become a natural part of your thought process, reinforcing a cycle of positive self-reflection and action that can help you navigate the ups and downs of daily life with greater ease and confidence.

Celebrating Uniqueness: Embracing Individuality

Imagine you're in an art gallery where every painting and sculpture is wildly different from the next. Each piece stands out because of its unique colors, shapes, and textures, making the gallery a rich tapestry of creativity and expression. Just like these works of art, every one of us has something special that makes us distinctly who we are. Valuing and celebrating this individuality isn't just about accepting differences; it's about reveling in them, knowing that these are what make you, well, you!

In a world that often seems to push us toward conformity—whether it's pressure from peers, images on social media, or even certain cultural expectations—it can feel easier sometimes just to blend in. But blending in is like dimming your own light. Think of it this way: When you try to be like everyone else, the world misses out on who you really are. Overcoming the urge to conform starts with recognizing your own value. It involves giving yourself permission to stand out and be proud of the qualities that make you different. This might mean embracing your quirky sense of humor, your unusual hobby, your amazing ability to quote movie lines, your athleticism, how you can mimic the voices of characters you've heard, your musical talents, or even your unorthodox way of solving problems.

Expressing yourself can be through the clothes you wear, the music you make, or the sketches in your notebook. All these are forms of self-expression that reflect different facets of your personality. Maybe you love bright, bold colors because they make you feel alive and vibrant, or perhaps you prefer writing poetry because it gives voice to your inner thoughts. Whatever it is, these forms of expression are important. They allow you to show the world who you are and help you connect with like-minded peers who appreciate and celebrate your individuality.

Finding these like-minded peers is actually a natural occurrence when you truly engage in what makes you feel happy and stop worrying about fitting in or conforming to those around you. Whether it's a book club, a gardening group, or a coding workshop, these are places where you can meet others who share your passions. In these spaces, you can freely express your thoughts and ideas, receive encouragement, and offer support. These connections can be incredibly validating, reinforcing that your unique interests and perspectives are valuable and appreciated.

Role Models: Finding Your Inspiration

Role models can be all around you. They might be historical figures who've changed the world, leaders in your community, or someone who looks like you or has maybe been through a struggle you are facing currently. They could be your family members, teachers, or coaches. What's important is how they make you feel, how they overcome challenges, and how they empower others. For instance, if you cherish creativity, a role model might be an artist or writer whose work encourages you to pursue your own creative projects. When you identify your role models, think about the specific actions they take or the attitudes they hold that you can integrate into your own life. It's not about becoming a replica of them, but rather, drawing inspiration from their journey to fuel your own.

Now, let's consider how you can be a role model for others. Think about the younger students at your school, your siblings, or even your peers. By acknowledging and practicing the traits you admire in your role models, you become a beacon for others. Remember how you looked up to the 5th or 6th graders when you were younger—how they were so amazing and cool? And if one of them talked to you, remember how special that made you feel? Well, you are now in a position to deliver a small happiness like that to the little ones! This doesn't mean you need to be perfect. In fact, laughing at yourself and showing how you navigate imperfections and setbacks can be incredibly inspiring. It's about living authentically and passionately, making choices that align with your values, and sharing what you learn along the way.

Remember, the influence of a role model can be powerful. They illuminate your path, inspire you to dream bigger, and provide the tools to reach those dreams. Just as importantly, by becoming a role model yourself, you contribute to a cycle of inspiration and growth that uplifts others around you. In this way, inspiration becomes a shared journey, where each of us has the opportunity to both teach and learn, to inspire and be inspired.

Let's wrap up this chapter with a brief reflection. We've explored a lot about building your inner strength and self-esteem, from understanding the power of positive self-talk to embracing your unique qualities. Each section provided tools to help you cultivate a stronger sense of self and a resilient mindset. As you move forward, carry these lessons with you as practical strategies to apply in your everyday life. Remember, confidence and self-esteem are like muscles—the more you work on them, the stronger they become.

Conclusion

As we close out this book, thereby ending this particular journey together, I want you to take a moment to reflect on everything we've explored in these pages. From the first flutterings of curiosity about puberty to the empowering knowledge you now hold, you've embarked on a remarkable path of discovery and growth. We've covered the essentials of puberty, the whirlwind of physical and emotional changes, the importance of maintaining health and hygiene, and the sometimes bumpy road of navigating friendships and relationships. We've also discussed the impact of social media on our self-image and how crucial it is to build a strong sense of self-confidence. Again, I urge you to stay off social media until you are at least in high school, but I would love for you to wait until you've graduated high school. You don't need it, and it adds nothing to learning the basics in the real world.

Each section of this book was designed to give you a holistic understanding of what it means to go through puberty. The journey is natural and entirely positive, a vibrant period of growth that shapes you into the person you're becoming. Remember, every experience of puberty is as unique as you are, and it's perfectly okay to reach out for help, ask endless questions, and share your thoughts and feelings.

I cannot stress enough how powerful knowledge is. Understanding the changes in your body and mind makes you approach puberty with confidence and self-assurance. This book is your friend and guide, a source you can always turn back to whenever you feel unsure or curious. Knowledge also gives you the power to take back your time from social media, empowering you to understand that it's meant to hold you captive while it feeds you partial, filtered, and edited information.

Now, as you continue to grow and navigate the exciting and sometimes challenging times ahead, keep asking questions and exploring. Talk about your experiences with friends or trusted adults, and use this book as a starting point for those conversations. It's a resource that grows with you, offering advice and comfort whenever you need it.

I wrote this book because I wanted to provide the kind of support and understanding I wish I had during my puberty journey. I hope it does the same for you, offering reassurance and a reminder that you are not alone. There's a whole community out here ready to support you, cheer you on, and celebrate every step you take. This community is in the real world—stay there for as long as you can.

Please feel free to share your thoughts on this book with others—friends, family, or even a review online. Your feedback is invaluable and helps others find the same support and understanding you've found here. Share your stories, too; your experiences and lessons are important and contribute to the ongoing conversation about growing up.

Thank you for sharing this journey with me. Remember, you are capable of navigating your way through puberty with grace and strength. I believe in you and your ability to shine brightly as you grow. Here's to your continued success and happiness on this incredible adventure of becoming your best self!

References

American Psychological Association. "Reducing Social Media Use Significantly Improves Body Image in Teens, Young Adults," February 23, 2023. https://www.apa.org/news/press/releases/2023/02/social-media-body-image.

Better Health Channel. "Teenagers and Communication," n.d. http://www.betterhealth.vic.gov.au/health/healthyliving/teenagers-and-communication.

Blakemore, Sarah-Jayne, Stephanie Burnett, and Ronald E. Dahl. "The Role of Puberty in the Developing Adolescent Brain." *Human Brain Mapping* 31, no. 6 (May 3, 2010): 926–33. https://doi.org/10.1002/hbm.21052.

Brennan, Dan. "Stages of Puberty." WebMD, February 12, 2023. https://www.webmd.com/children/ss/slideshow-puberty-stages.

Claney, Carley. "Understanding How Hormonal Changes Impact Emotional Health for Teens." Relational Psych, July 18, 2023. https://www.relationalpsych.group/articles/understanding-how-hormonal-changes-impact-emotional-health-for-teens.

Common Sense Education. "Great Online Communities for Kids and Teens," n.d. https://www.commonsense.org/education/lists/great-online-communities-for-kids-and-teens.

Dove. "The Importance of Individuality and Uniqueness," May 19, 2020. https://www.dove.com/uk/dove-self-esteem-project/help-for-parents/respecting-and-looking-after-yourself/individuality.html.

Ehmke, Rachel. "How Using Social Media Affects Teenagers." Child Mind Institute, n.d. https://childmind.org/article/how-using-social-media-affects-teenagers/.

Fourcassier, Sarah, Mélanie Douziech, Paula Pérez-López, and Londa Schiebinger. "Menstrual Products: A Comparable Life Cycle Assessment." *Cleaner Environmental Systems* 7 (December 1, 2022): 100096. https://doi.org/10.1016/j.cesys.2022.100096.

Garey, Juliann. "Raising Girls With Healthy Self-Esteem." Child Mind Institute, n.d. https://childmind.org/article/raising-girls-with-healthy-self-esteem/.

Holmes, Melisa. "How to Insert a Tampon." Tampax, n.d. https://tampax.com/en-us/tampon-truths/how-to-insert-a-tampon/.

Lidyard, Nicole. "Your Teen's Growth Spurt: How to Fuel It Right." University Hospitals, April 22, 2019. https://www.uhhospitals.org/blog/articles/2019/04/teen-growth-spurt-how-to-fuel-it-right.

Marcin, Ashley. "Stages of Puberty: A Guide for Males and Females." Healthline, December 1, 2015. https://www.healthline.com/health/parenting/stages-of-puberty.

McLaughlin, Jessica E. "Puberty in Girls—Puberty in Girls." Merck Manual Consumer Version, September 2022. https://www.merckmanuals.com/home/women-s-health-issues/biology-of-the-female-reproductive-system/puberty-in-girls.

Nariman, Julie. "How to Help Teens Set Effective Goals (Tips & Templates)." Big Life Journal, January 4, 2024. https://biglifejournal.com/blogs/blog/guide-effective-goal-setting-teens-template-worksheet.

Nemours TeensHealth. "Hygiene Basics (for Teens)," n.d.

Period.org. "The Launch Pad Education," n.d. https://period-action.org/education.

Pickhardt, Carl E. "Adolescence and Falling In Love." Psychology Today, June 18, 2022. https://www.psychologytoday.com/us/blog/surviving-your-childs-adolescence/201206/adolescence-and-falling-in-love.

Raising Children Network. "Friends and Friendships: Pre-Teens and Teenagers," March 12, 2024. https://raisingchildren.net.au/pre-teens/behaviour/peers-friends-trends/teen-friendships.

ScienceDaily. "Physical Activity Can Help Mental Health in Pre-Teen Years," March 1, 2023. https://www.sciencedaily.com/releases/2023/03/230301210307.htm.

Social Media Victims Law Center. "Social Media's Effect on Self-Esteem: How Does It Affect Teens?," n.d. https://socialmediavictims.org/mental-health/self-esteem/.

SocialWorkersToolbox.com. "Healthy Body Image: Information & Interactive Activities," May 16, 2016. https://www.socialworkerstoolbox.com/body-image-information-interactive-activities/.

The Pathway 2 Success. "How to Teach Positive Self-Talk," June 15, 2017. https://www.thepathway2success.com/how-to-teach-positive-self-talk/.

The Soccer Mom Blog. "100 Strong Female Role Models That ALL Kids Should Know About," May 6, 2019. https://thesoccermomblog.com/100-strong-female-role-models/.

Thompson, Betsy. "The Best Period Tracking Apps for Young Girls." *Protect Young Eyes* (blog), October 8, 2020. https://protectyoungeyes.com/the-best-period-tracking-apps-for-young-girls/.

Tilly's Life Center. "The Mental Health Benefits of Journaling for Teens," October 25, 2022. https://tillyslifecenter.org/2022/10/25/journaling-for-teens-mental-health-resources/.

UNICEF. "Cyberbullying: What Is It and How to Stop It," n.d. https://www.unicef.org/end-violence/how-to-stop-cyberbullying.

USC Annenberg. "Critical Media Project," n.d. http://annenberg.usc.edu/research/critical-media-project.

Vallejo, Michael. "101 Effective Coping Skills for Teens." Mental Health Center Kids, September 2, 2022. https://mentalhealthcenterkids.com/blogs/articles/coping-skills-for-teens.

Westgate Resorts. "Digital Detox for Kids [31 Tips and Activities Included]," September 19, 2023. https://www.westgateresorts.com.

Wier, Kirsten. "Improving Sibling Relationships." American Psychological Association, March 1, 2022. https://www.apa.org/monitor/2022/03/feature-sibling-relationships.

Made in United States
Cleveland, OH
15 June 2025